T0021739

SUPER-EASY
INSTANT POT COOKBOOK

Super-Easy
INSTANT POT COOKBOOK

QUICK PREP • ONE-POT
5-INGREDIENT • 30-MINUTE RECIPES

JANET A. ZIMMERMAN

ROCKRIDGE
PRESS

Copyright © 2022 by Rockridge Press, Oakland, California

No part of this publication may be reproduced, stored in a retrieval system, or transmitted in any form or by any means, electronic, mechanical, photocopying, recording, scanning, or otherwise, except as permitted under Sections 107 or 108 of the 1976 United States Copyright Act, without the prior written permission of the Publisher. Requests to the Publisher for permission should be addressed to the Permissions Department, Rockridge Press, 1955 Broadway, Suite 400, Oakland, CA 94612.

Limit of Liability/Disclaimer of Warranty: The Publisher and the author make no representations or warranties with respect to the accuracy or completeness of the contents of this work and specifically disclaim all warranties, including without limitation warranties of fitness for a particular purpose. No warranty may be created or extended by sales or promotional materials. The advice and strategies contained herein may not be suitable for every situation. This work is sold with the understanding that the Publisher is not engaged in rendering medical, legal, or other professional advice or services. If professional assistance is required, the services of a competent professional person should be sought. Neither the Publisher nor the author shall be liable for damages arising herefrom. The fact that an individual, organization, or website is referred to in this work as a citation and/or potential source of further information does not mean that the author or the Publisher endorses the information the individual, organization, or website may provide or recommendations they/it may make. Further, readers should be aware that websites listed in this work may have changed or disappeared between when this work was written and when it is read.

For general information on our other products and services or to obtain technical support, please contact our Customer Care Department within the United States at (866) 744-2665, or outside the United States at (510) 253-0500.

Rockridge Press publishes its books in a variety of electronic and print formats. Some content that appears in print may not be available in electronic books, and vice versa.

TRADEMARKS: Rockridge Press and the Rockridge Press logo are trademarks or registered trademarks of Callisto Media Inc. and/or its affiliates, in the United States and other countries, and may not be used without written permission. All other trademarks are the property of their respective owners. Rockridge Press is not associated with any product or vendor mentioned in this book.

Interior and Cover Designer: Alan Carr & Lisa Realmuto
Art Producer: Maya Melenchuk
Editor: Van Van Cleave
Production Manager: David Zapanta

Author photo courtesy of Mast Photography. Photography © Darren Muir, cover, pp. ii, vi, ix, x, 20, 28, 36, 48, 50, 54, 59, 70, 85, 92, 126, 135, 138, 151, 156; © Hélene Dujardin, pp. 16, 75, 142; © Laura Flippen, pp. 38, 88, 108, 144; © Marija Vidal, pp. 94, 106, 122.

Paperback ISBN: 978-1-63878-047-2
eBook ISBN: 978-1-63878-262-9
R0

AS ALWAYS, TO DAVE,
*who makes developing recipes much more fun
and who almost always cleans up after me.*

CONTENTS

INTRODUCTION

A funny thing happened when I was working on this book. The schedule was such that I was developing and testing recipes in the weeks leading up to Thanksgiving. I took most of the holiday week off so that my partner, Dave, and I could plan, shop, and cook for the guests we'd invited for dinner.

It was fun—we both like cooking, and we like cooking together—and dinner was delicious. On the other hand, after two days of cooking, I was exhausted. My back hurt. We ran the dishwasher five times in those two days, then twice the day after Thanksgiving.

Of course, it's always like that on holidays, and I knew what to expect. Somehow, though, it seemed like a lot more work this year (maybe I'm just getting old!). As I surveyed the kitchenful of dirty dishes the morning after, it occurred to me what the difference was. After weeks of preparing Instant Pot dinners that required very few ingredients and little prep work, that cooked quickly, and that left very few dirty dishes, I was spoiled.

It's no secret by now what a difference the Instant Pot has made to home cooks around the world. I've written four pressure cooker books—two specifically for the Instant Pot—and edited or compiled three more, so I know how popular Instant Pot cooking has become. Still, it can seem intimidating. Traditionally, pressure cooking was known for long-cooking batches of beans and grains or tough cuts of meats. If that's not your thing, it may seem that an Instant Pot can't offer you much.

I'm here to say that nothing can be further from the truth. With the versatility of the Instant Pot, you can cook just about anything—and cook it faster with less cleanup. Stick with me, and you'll learn how.

Truth be told, no matter how much I love creating elaborate dishes, there's a lot to be said for having an arsenal of fast, easy recipes that don't yield a sink full of dirty dishes, a grease-splattered stovetop, and a messy oven.

And that's what this book provides—recipes for breakfasts, dinners, and desserts that make cooking easy in a variety of ways. Some require only a handful of ingredients (five, plus salt, pepper, and oil); some take only five minutes of prep time; some can be made from start to finish in 30 minutes; some even hit more than one category! There are some longer-cooking dishes with more ingredients, but those are almost all complete meals in one pot, so cleanup is a snap.

I developed most of these recipes specifically for this book. A few of the recipes are from my previous books or other experienced cookbook authors, which I've adapted. They include a mix of flavors, regional and international cuisine styles, and ingredients.

Maybe you love to cook; maybe you like cooking when you have the time; maybe you only tolerate it because you must. Whatever your circumstances, I hope the recipes gathered here make your kitchen time more fun, or at least less stressful!

Super-Easy Instant Pot Cooking

I f you're a busy cook who still wants to prepare tasty, healthy meals for yourself or your family, you're in the right place. Before diving into the recipes, let's spend a little time exploring the Instant Pot and learning how it can make cooking easier and faster.

Hands-Off Cooking for Busy People

It's no secret that the Instant Pot has revolutionized cooking for users all over the world. Home cooks have discovered that pressure cooking is fast, safe, and reliable. The Instant Pot is an ideal appliance for busy cooks, especially parents in charge of preparing meals for their families.

Even so, some people are hesitant about diving into Instant Pot cooking. Maybe you've heard that it's hard to use, that you can never tell when your food is cooked because you can't check on it, or that it's only for long-cooking dishes such as beans and grains or giant cuts of meat.

But stick with me, and you'll discover that with a bit of practice, the Instant Pot is easy to use. You'll learn how to get great results every time from the "magic" sealed pot, whether you're cooking breakfast, dinner, or desserts. You'll see that it's just as useful for quick weeknight meals as it is for weekend pot roasts.

Even if you're an experienced Instant Pot user, you'll find that with this book, your cooking will get easier and quicker, with delicious, mostly hands-off dishes as a result. There are several approaches to streamlining dinner prep, and this book takes advantage of them all. None of the recipes require any cooking outside the Instant Pot (although a few offer that as an option). Some recipes can be made in 30 minutes from start to finish. Some require only five ingredients (and most require no more than 10). Others are complete meals made entirely in the Instant Pot, with no extra bowls to clean. Quick prep dishes are ready to start cooking in five minutes. And many recipes even hit more than one of these categories.

So, if you're looking for dishes that are super easy, mostly hands-off, usually fast, and always delicious, read on.

Getting to Know Your Pot

If you're a new Instant Pot user, you might be intimidated by all its parts and controls. Don't worry! The Instant Pot is easy to use with a little practice. Let's take a quick look at the appliance itself.

HOW THE INSTANT POT WORKS

If you're not familiar with how a pressure cooker works, it can seem like magic, but it's really science. In basic terms, pressure cooking is possible because the boiling point of liquid depends on the atmospheric pressure. In a conventional pot, water-based cooking liquids will never get above 212°F (100°C). As the water in a pot boils, it turns to steam, and the steam dissipates—even with a lid on. But in the sealed chamber of a pressure cooker, the water that turns to steam can't escape, which increases the pressure in the pot. The higher pressure means that more energy is necessary for the water to boil, so the boiling point rises. Thus, in the Instant Pot under pressure, the cooking temperature ranges from about 230°F (110°C) to 245°F (118°C), meaning that foods cook more quickly than in a traditional pot on the stove.

And the Instant Pot is more than just a pressure cooker. You can sauté, sear, and simmer foods using the Sauté function; pressure steam vegetables or fish; or make yogurt. The Instant Pot also functions as a slow cooker.

Whether you're cooking under pressure or using one of the non-pressure functions, multiple features make the Instant Pot reliably safe to use. The primary safety features include a safety lid lock and a sensor that ensures that the lid is in a safe position for pressure cooking; a pressure regulator, which ensures that the working pressure stays below the safety limit; and an automatic temperature control, which regulates the cooking temperature based on the type of program selected.

PARTS

Most of the parts of the Instant Pot are the same, regardless of the model, but there are some slight variations. For a complete guide, check your manual.

- **Base:** This contains the heating element, which is completely enclosed.

- **Control panel:** This varies from model to model. In the most popular model, the Duo, it consists of selection buttons and a display screen that counts down the time for the program you're using. You'll use it to choose the cooking function, set the pressure level and time, and start and cancel cooking when done.

- **Lid:** Designed to lock into place, the lid will seal completely when pressure cooking. It contains a sealing ring, steam release handle, and float valve.

- **Sealing ring:** Made of silicone, this fits securely under the edge of the lid.

- **Steam release handle:** This is used to release the pressure after cooking. In some models, it has to be moved from "sealing" to "release;" in others, the default position is "sealing."

- **Float valve:** This pin-lock mechanism rises when pressure is reached and falls when pressure is released. It prevents the lid from being opened while the unit is under pressure.

- **Inner pot:** Made of stainless steel, the removable inner pot fits into the base and is where the actual cooking occurs.

- **Condensation cup:** Available on some models, this clips into place on the outside of the appliance to collect any moisture that condenses during cooking.

CONTROLS

As mentioned above, the control panel on the Instant Pot varies slightly depending on the model. It has selections for all the main cooking functions—Pressure Cook, Sauté, Slow Cook, and (on some models) Yogurt—plus preset selections for pressure cooking some specific foods, such as grains, beans, or meat. Depending on your model, you'll select the cooking function by pressing a button or using a dial or touch screen.

- **Pressure Cook (or Manual):** This is the function used most frequently in this book. After selecting Pressure Cook, you'll adjust the pressure to High or Low (in all models except the LUX) and set the time. In some models, cooking begins automatically; in some, you'll press a Start button.

- **Steam:** This is a specialized pressure-cooking function designed for steaming foods over water on a trivet or in a steaming basket.

- **Sauté:** Used to simmer sauces, you can adjust the heat level of this function to Low, Medium, or High (labeled Less, Normal, and More on some models). After you're finished cooking, select Cancel to stop cooking.

PRESET PROS AND CONS

With the wealth of cooking selections ("Smart Programs") on the Instant Pot, it can be overwhelming to try to decide which one to use. Here's a quick rundown of what they do.

Poultry, Beans/Chili, Soup, Meat: This is the majority of the presets, and all cook on High pressure and with three default preset times, although the time can also be customized.

Multigrain: This function has a presoaking time before it starts coming to pressure.

Rice: Designed for white rice only, this cooks on low pressure. The time is predetermined depending on the amount of rice in the pot.

Steam: This function heats continuously, while the others cycle on and off; thus, it gets hotter faster.

With the exception of the Steam setting, the recipes in this book do not use any of the Smart Programs. There are a couple of reasons for this. First, different models and sizes have different programs, and I want to spare you the frustration of calling for a program that your machine doesn't have. Second, the times in my recipes don't always align with the preset times of the Smart Programs, so you'd have to adjust the time anyway.

That being said, it can be worth the time to familiarize yourself with your machine's Smart Programs (check your manual for details). If they align with the dishes you like to cook, they can be a handy, quick way to get your Instant Pot cooking with less work up front.

The Easy Guide to Using Your Instant Pot

Though the recipes in the book are varied, they almost all follow the same general cooking plan. Once you familiarize yourself with the following steps, you'll be well on your way to becoming an Instant Pot pro.

1. **Precook select ingredients.** Although I try to keep this to a minimum, a few recipes will require sautéing vegetables or browning meat before pressure cooking. You can do this right in the pot, using the Sauté function.

2. **Add liquid.** Liquid is essential for pressure cooking, so you will need to add water, broth, or other liquid to the pot. (Because meats and vegetables release liquid as they cook, you don't always need much.) Be sure to scrape up any browned bits of food from the bottom of the pot if you've sautéed or seared to start. When steaming foods or cooking pot-in-pot, you'll add water (usually 1 cup) to the inner pot and place the food in a steamer basket or on the trivet.

3. **Lock the lid.** After adding any remaining ingredients, check the lid to make sure that the sealing ring is in place and seated correctly, then lock the lid in place. Make sure that the steam release knob is in the sealed position. If it's not, the pot won't build pressure.

4. **Set the cooking functions.** To cook with the Pressure Cook (or Manual) function or on Steam, set the pressure level (High or Low), then enter the cook time. Some models have a Start button; some start on their own a few seconds after the cook time is set.

5. **Release pressure.** After cooking, release the pressure according to the recipe's instructions. To quick-release, press Cancel and move the steam release knob to the Vent position. (Some models will have a steam release button instead.) To release the pressure naturally, simply wait for the pressure to come down on its own—usually 15 to 20 minutes. Some recipes call for natural release for a set amount of time, followed by a quick release of the remaining pressure.

6. **Finish cooking.** In a few of the recipes, you may need to repeat the previous pressure-cooking steps to cook additional ingredients separately (such as Hoisin Beef and Broccoli, page 125). In some recipes (such as Pasta Primavera, page 80), you'll add some ingredients after pressure cooking—cream or cheese, for instance—or simmer for a few minutes to reduce a sauce.

7. **Clean up.** Unplug the Instant Pot and remove the inner pot and lid. Refer to your manual for cleaning instructions.

Scaling Up and Down

Most recipes in this book make 4 to 6 servings. If you want to make a smaller or larger amount, it's not difficult to scale recipes up or down if you can do a little basic math. However, as a rule of thumb, never change the amount of water in the bottom of the pot when you're steaming food on the trivet or cooking pot-in-pot. And I also suggest sticking to doubling or halving recipes, because the math is easier.

ADJUSTING RECIPES FOR HIGH-ALTITUDE COOKING

If you paid attention in science class, you'll remember that the higher the altitude, the lower the atmospheric pressure. For cooking, this means that the higher up you are, the lower the boiling point of water, and the faster it will evaporate. While the sealed interior of the Instant Pot helps to make up for the lower atmospheric pressure, you'll still want to adjust cooking times if you live in the mountains. The Ultra and MAX models can be set to adjust automatically for high altitudes, but if you have a different model, you'll need to increase cooking times by 5 percent for every 1,000 feet above 2,000 feet. For short cooking times, there will be virtually no difference, but for longer times, some adjustment is necessary. For instance, if you're cooking Beef and Potato Stew (page 66) at 5,000 feet, you'd increase the cooking time for the beef from 22 to 25 minutes.

SCALING UP

Doubling a recipe is relatively straightforward, with a few caveats. First, *never* fill the inner pot more than two-thirds full; a full pot is a dangerous pot. Second, unless you're a very experienced Instant Pot cook, don't try to double a soup or stew recipe—all the extra liquid will take a long time to come to pressure, so your soup will almost always overcook. Third, if you want to double something cooked in a baking dish, you're best off just making two batches. Other than that, if you have a big enough pot, just double all the ingredients. The cooking times generally won't change, except if there's a very short cooking time (under 5 minutes). The extra ingredients may cause the pot to take longer to come to pressure, which can mean overcooking. Adjust accordingly.

SCALING DOWN

Scaling down is both easier and trickier. It's easier because you don't have to worry about overfilling the inner pot. It's trickier because, although in most cases you can just cut the recipe ingredients by half, there are two things you have to watch for: One is liquid. Remember that with pressure cooking, you need liquid boiling to reach pressure. You don't need much, but the total liquid should never be less than ¼ to ½ cup, depending on the ingredients—meats and vegetables exude water as they cook, so you can often get by with the smaller amount. The other thing is fat. You shouldn't reduce the amount of oil or fat when you're sautéing or browning ingredients; always make sure you have enough to cover the bottom of the pot. The cooking time will usually remain the same, but with a smaller volume inside the pot, it will take less time to come to pressure. You may occasionally need to increase the cooking time to account for that.

Equipment Essentials

I tried to make sure the recipes for this book didn't require a cabinet full of extra equipment, but there are a few items that will come in handy as you cook.

- **Baking dish:** My go-to dish is a ceramic, straight-sided soufflé dish, but any heatproof dish or bowl will work, as long it holds 6 cups and fits inside the inner pot with at least ¼ inch of space all around.

- **Individual ramekins or custard cups:** You'll use these for some breakfast and dessert recipes; they should hold about 8 ounces (1 cup).

- **Silicone egg mold:** This nonstick pan contains indentations for 6 to 8 eggs, but they're also great for muffin bites.

- **Immersion blender:** Also called a stick blender, this is great for pureeing soups or sauces.

- **Hand mixer:** This makes desserts much easier, although you can sometimes get by with just a whisk.

- **Tall trivet:** Though this is not essential, it can come in handy if you want to cook one food in the pot and steam something else over it at the same time.

Other useful pieces of equipment include sturdy tongs, a long wooden or silicone spoon, a heavy whisk, and silicone finger mitts for removing the inner pot.

THE JOY OF FREEZER FEASTS

If you're the type who likes to plan and prep meals in advance, you may want to take advantage of your freezer for make-ahead meals. Some recipes lend themselves to being assembled in a zip-top freezer bag, frozen, and then thawed and cooked later in the week or month. The best candidates for this are recipes that call for meats cooked in a sauce, or soups and stews without rice, potatoes, or pasta. For instance, the filling ingredients for Shredded Italian Chicken Sandwiches (page 96) work great when prepped this way, as do the beef and sauce from Hoisin Beef and Broccoli (page 125). Casserole dishes can also sometimes be assembled right in the baking dish and then frozen. (One thing to remember: If your ingredients have been frozen and thawed, never refreeze them.)

However, in most cases, I don't recommend cooking from frozen in the Instant Pot for a couple of reasons. First, frozen foods retain the best texture when thawed as slowly as possible. Cooking from frozen can result in spongy, chewy meat and mushy vegetables. Second, because frozen food takes so long to come to pressure, it can mess with the timing of your recipes. Instead, plan ahead. If you transfer your freezer meal to the refrigerator the night or morning before you plan to cook it, you'll be all set when you get home from work.

Still, if you forget this thawing step, all is not lost. You can always speed-thaw your dinner by placing the bag in a basin of barely lukewarm water until the contents begin to thaw. At that point, transfer the contents to the Instant Pot and warm the ingredients on the Sauté setting until the liquid is warmed up to room temperature. Continue with the recipe as written, increasing the cooking time by about 20 percent.

Stocking the Super-Easy Instant Pot Kitchen

To make your cooking easier, it's helpful to have a pantry of frequently used ingredients on hand. I've tried whenever possible to include these in several recipes, so they'll get lots of use. None of them are exotic or hard to find; you might even have some of them already.

REFRIGERATOR STAPLES

Though refrigerated items don't last forever, there are several items with long shelf lives that should live in your refrigerator.

- **Dairy:** I have included a bunch of dairy-free recipes in this book, but if you don't have dietary restrictions, you'll get a lot of use out of butter, heavy cream, whole milk, and half-and-half.

- **Cheeses:** Cheddar, Swiss, mozzarella, and Parmesan (or similar cheeses) make frequent appearances in my recipes. Buying good-quality shredded cheese will save time, although you won't get quite as good a selection as you will with shredding your own from block cheese.

- **Eggs:** Eggs have a very long life in the refrigerator and are invaluable in breakfast recipes and baking.

- **Cooked bacon and diced ham:** Cured meats will last for weeks.

- **Sturdy vegetables:** Carrots, cabbage, and celery are examples of vegetables to stock up on.

- **Delicate vegetables:** Items like fresh herbs, spinach, and other leafy greens should be purchased as needed.

FREEZER STAPLES

For easy cooking, nothing beats a well-stocked freezer. Plan to have the following items on hand:

- **Individually Quick Frozen (IQF) shrimp and fish fillets:** Shrimp and fish can sometimes be cooked right from frozen or thawed quickly for almost-instant dinners.

- **Frozen vegetables:** Frozen breakfast potatoes, peas, corn, and various mixed vegetables can save you tons of time in the kitchen. You'll usually want to thaw these before using, but they all thaw very quickly.

- **Frozen minced garlic and ginger:** These time-saving aromatics are worth their weight in gold.

PANTRY STAPLES

Sturdy vegetables stored at room temperature, canned goods, jarred sauces, and spice mixtures are a godsend for the busy cook, and these ingredients will see frequent use in this book.

- **Potatoes, onions, and garlic:** Stored in a cool, dark place, these will last for weeks.

- **Canned beans:** Pintos, black beans, chickpeas, and white beans are all great to have on hand.

- **Rice:** Long-grain white rice is my standby, but I sometimes use brown rice as well. Arborio is good for risotto and rice pudding.

- **Pasta:** Shapes like farfalle, penne, shells, and rotini are preferable to long, thin shapes like spaghetti and linguine, which can stick together in the pressure cooker.

- **Canned diced tomatoes:** I like fire-roasted, but any type will work.

- **Prepared sauces:** Sauces such as soy, teriyaki, marinara, Thai curry paste, pesto, mustard, salsa, hot pepper, and chili-garlic add instant flavor to many dishes.

- **Oils and vinegars:** Vegetable oil, extra-virgin olive oil, wine vinegar, balsamic vinegar, and apple cider vinegar are the types I use most often.

- **Stocks or broths:** Low-sodium chicken stock and vegetable broth are great for pressure cooking; seafood stock can also be delicious.

- **Salt and pepper:** I use Diamond Crystal kosher salt in the majority of my recipes; if you use fine salt (table salt like Morton's or fine sea salt), use half as much. Freshly ground pepper has much more flavor than preground.

- **Spice mixtures:** Using well-blended spice mixtures such as curry powder, chili powder, and apple or pumpkin pie spice can save time and space in your spice cabinet.

5 Steps to Make Instant Pot Cooking Super Easy

This book's recipes provide a great start if you want to make cooking easy and fast, but there are many ways to streamline meal preparation, making dinner or breakfast even simpler. Here are a few of my favorite tips:

- **Embrace the freezer aisle:** With a few adjustments, you can often swap frozen vegetables for fresh in Instant Pot recipes without sacrificing flavor or texture. Frozen shrimp and fish are tailor-made for the Instant Pot, and frozen minced ginger and garlic cubes are also huge time-savers.

- **Look for precut produce:** Almost every produce section has shelves of chopped, peeled vegetables, from broccoli and cauliflower florets to bags of "baby" carrots, deli containers of chopped onions or celery, and cubed squash. Though they aren't as durable as whole vegetables, they're a welcome convenience.

- **Prep ingredients ahead:** If you can't find or don't want to purchase chopped vegetables, you can still save time by prepping ingredients such as onions, bell peppers, or herbs for several meals at once. Taking a bit of time to separate large packages of meat and poultry now can also mean an easier meal later.

- **Stock up on sauces:** A few well-made commercial sauces such as salsa, curry paste, barbecue sauce, or marinara can give your dishes lots of flavor with very little work. Even after opening, most will last for a few weeks in the refrigerator.

- **Choose the right cuts of meat:** Many cuts of pork, beef, and chicken can be cooked in the Instant Pot, but don't assume you can switch one for another in a given recipe. Pork tenderloin, for instance, cooks much more quickly than shoulder cuts, and chicken breasts cook differently from thighs.

Troubleshooting

The Instant Pot is generally dependable and rarely malfunctions. However, as you become accustomed to pressure cooking, you may encounter a few problems. These are almost always easy to solve. Let's go over a few common ones.

- **It's been 20 minutes, and pressure cooking hasn't started:** If you're cooking a large amount of food or frozen or cold liquids, it may take up to 30 minutes for pressure to build. This delay is caused by one of two culprits: First, make sure the steam release knob is in the sealed position. Then, check to make sure the sealing ring is correctly seated and undamaged.

- **Steam is leaking out from around the lid:** This is usually caused by a missing, damaged, or incorrectly inserted sealing ring. It may also be that the lid was not closed correctly. Release any pressure, remove the lid and ring, and check them.

- **I got a Burn message:** Instant Pots are configured with a heat sensor in the bottom of the unit. When the pot overheats, the Burn warning is displayed (in some models, this is "Ovht" or "Food Burn") and the pot shuts down. It's usually triggered when there isn't enough liquid and pressure doesn't build. To avoid it, make sure the lid is sealed correctly, that you have enough liquid, and that there is no food stuck to the bottom of the pot. If you get a Burn notice, scrape up any stuck food, make sure there is enough liquid, and—most important—let the pot cool down before continuing.

- **The float valve isn't rising:** Food particles sometimes spatter and collect on the underside of the float valve, which prevents it from rising. Always be sure to clean the valve after each use, and if stuck, remove it from the lid, thoroughly clean it, and reattach.

- **I can't close the lid:** If you can't lock the lid in place at the start of cooking, check to make sure the sealing ring is properly set. If you stop cooking to add ingredients, you may need to let the contents cool a bit before the lid will lock in place to continue cooking.

- **I can't open the lid:** If you can't open the lid after cooking, it's usually one of two issues. First, the float valve sometimes gets stuck. If it does, use a long utensil to gently push it down. The other problem is that the pot is still pressurized. Make sure the pressure completely drops, and let the contents cool for a few minutes. The lid should open, but be careful to open it slowly and away from you.

5 FAST-AND-EASY FAVORITES

Naturally, I think all the recipes in this book are wonderful. But if you need some persuading that the Instant Pot can turn out quick and easy dishes that are delicious as well, here's a preview of what's to come.

1. **Chorizo Chili (page 55):** A handful of ingredients and 30 minutes is all it takes for this flavorful, healthy meal in a pot. Bonus: There's almost no prep.

2. **Beef Stroganoff (page 118):** This elegant entrée is ready in under an hour and even includes the noodles, so you don't need to dirty an extra pan.

3. **Shredded Italian Chicken Sandwiches (page 96):** For a casual family supper, these quick, tasty sandwiches will soon become a weeknight favorite.

4. **Pasta Primavera (page 80):** One of the Instant Pot's greatest tricks is cooking pasta and sauce all at once, which not only saves time, but also cuts way down on cleanup. This tasty, meatless entrée is ready in less than 45 minutes.

5. **Key Lime Mousse (page 136):** Dessert has never been easier than this five-ingredient creamy mousse that's elegant enough for company.

The Recipes in This Book

The recipes in this book were developed for any (5-quart or larger) Instant Pot model. Most recipes will make 4 to 6 servings. (Some of the recipes can be cut in half to fit in the Instant Pot Mini; see instructions for scaling down on page 8.) Most take less than an hour and require fewer than 10 ingredients. They're easy enough for busy weeknights and will yield delicious results that your whole family will love.

To make it easy to select recipes that fit into your schedule and match your cooking style, every recipe is flagged with at least one of the following "Super-Easy" tags:

- **30-Minute:** These recipes can be prepped, cooked, and finished in 30 minutes or less.

- **One-Pot Meal:** In dishes with this label, all of the ingredients of a meal—protein, vegetables, and (often) starch—are cooked together in the Instant Pot. As a bonus, there are no extra bowls or pans for super-simple cleanup.

- **Quick Prep:** These recipes require 5 minutes or less of prep time.

- **5-Ingredient:** These are dishes that call for 5 or fewer ingredients, aside from a few "freebies"—water, salt, pepper, and oil or cooking spray.

In addition, to help you find recipes that fit your dietary requirements, the recipes are also flagged with two dietary labels: Dairy-Free and Vegetarian.

All the recipes feature a breakdown of the time required, which includes prep time, sautéing time when appropriate, time under pressure, any cooling and/or chilling time needed, and the total time. The total time also includes the average time it takes the pot to come to pressure—which is often less than 10 minutes—as well as the time to quick-release pressure—which is usually about a minute. The prep time includes time to prepare the ingredients for cooking and any time necessary for finishing the dish after pressure cooking. Though I've tried to be as accurate as possible, several factors, such as the temperature of liquid ingredients, the size of cut ingredients, and the material of your cooking vessels (for steamed dishes), can affect the cooking time.

To calculate the prep times, I've assumed that you'll be buying many vegetables already chopped, either fresh or frozen, and preshredded cheeses. If instead you chop onions and bell peppers, mince garlic or ginger, or shred cheese, your prep times will increase. On the plus side, you'll save money and improve your knife skills.

Finally, most of the recipes are followed by tips, which include variations and substitutions, "flavor-boost" steps or ingredients, and make-ahead/freezer instructions.

I hope you have as much fun making these recipes as I did developing them, and that they'll inspire you to head into the kitchen. Let's get cooking!

Breakfast and Brunch

Vegetable Tortilla Española

5-INGREDIENT • DAIRY-FREE • QUICK PREP • VEGETARIAN

Serves 6

Prep time:
5 minutes

Sauté:
6 minutes

Pressure cook:
20 minutes

Release:
Natural
(10 minutes),
then quick

Cooling time:
10 minutes

Total time:
1 hour

Spanish tortillas are flat omelets similar to Italian frittatas, usually filled with potatoes and sometimes other vegetables. Served warm, they make a delicious, hearty breakfast; in Spain, they're often cut into bite-size pieces and served at room temperature as part of a tapas spread. Either way, they're delicious!

Cooking spray

1 tablespoon olive oil

½ cup thinly sliced Yukon Gold potato

½ cup thinly sliced zucchini

½ cup thinly sliced yellow onion

6 large eggs

½ teaspoon kosher salt

¼ teaspoon freshly ground black pepper

1 cup water

1. Mist a 6-inch baking dish or cake pan with cooking spray.

2. Select Sauté and adjust the heat to Medium. Pour in the olive oil. When the oil is hot, add the potato, zucchini, and onion. Cook, stirring occasionally, for about 6 minutes, or until the onions begin to brown and the potatoes crisp. Press Cancel. Transfer the cooked vegetables to the prepared baking dish.

3. In a large bowl, whisk together the eggs, salt, and pepper. Pour the egg mixture over the vegetables. Cover the top of the baking dish with aluminum foil.

4. Pour 1 cup of water into the inner pot and insert a trivet with handles. Place the baking dish on the trivet.

5. Lock the lid in place. Select Pressure Cook or Manual; adjust the pressure to High and the time to 20 minutes.

6. When cooking is complete, let the pressure release naturally for 10 minutes, then quick-release any remaining pressure.

7. Remove the lid and lift out the baking dish and trivet. Uncover the tortilla and let it cool for 10 minutes on the trivet, then cut it into 6 wedges. Serve warm.

EVEN EASIER: To save a little prep time, use thawed frozen hash browns or home fries instead of the sliced potatoes.

Per Serving (1 wedge): Calories: 122; Fat: 9.5g; Protein: 7g; Total carbohydrates: 4g; Fiber: 0.5g; Sugar: 1g; Sodium: 169mg

Creamy Banana-Nut Steel-Cut Oats

ONE-POT MEAL · QUICK PREP · VEGETARIAN

Serves 6

Prep time:
5 minutes

Pressure cook:
4 minutes

Release:
Natural

Cooling time:
5 minutes

Total time:
40 minutes

Delicious, filling steel-cut oats are a breeze to make in an Instant Pot. This recipe combines them with bananas and walnuts for a warming breakfast on cool mornings.

3½ cups whole milk
1 cup steel-cut oats
2 bananas, sliced
¼ cup packed light brown sugar

1 teaspoon sea salt
1 teaspoon vanilla extract
½ teaspoon ground cinnamon
½ cup chopped walnuts

1. In the inner pot, combine the milk, oats, bananas, brown sugar, salt, vanilla, and cinnamon. Stir all the ingredients together.

2. Lock the lid into place. Select Pressure Cook or Manual; adjust the pressure to High and the time to 4 minutes.

3. When cooking is complete, let the pressure release naturally for 10 minutes (as the oats will continue cooking during this time).

4. Remove the lid, stir the oats, and let stand for 5 minutes to thicken.

5. Stir in the walnuts and serve.

VARIATION: Instead of bananas and walnuts, use finely chopped apple and sliced almonds.

Per Serving: Calories: 323; Fat: 13g; Protein: 10g; Total carbohydrates: 44g; Fiber: 4.5g; Sugar: 22g; Sodium: 457mg

Classic Diner Breakfast Casserole

5-INGREDIENT

Serves 4 for brunch, 6 for breakfast

Prep time:
10 minutes

Pressure cook:
18 minutes

Release:
Quick

Cooling time:
10 minutes

Total time:
45 minutes

This casserole combines the best of a classic diner breakfast—bacon, eggs, and home fries. Frozen potatoes with peppers and onions (Ore-Ida's Potatoes O'Brien are the best-known brand) add extra flavor, but plain frozen hash browns will also work here. Be sure the potatoes are thawed before using, or the water exuded as they melt will make the eggs runny.

Cooking spray or oil

2 cups frozen potatoes, peppers, and onions, thawed

2 cups shredded cheddar cheese (about 4 ounces), divided

2 cups chopped cooked bacon (about 8 slices)

6 large eggs

⅔ cup half-and-half or whole milk

½ teaspoon kosher salt

¼ teaspoon freshly ground black pepper

1 cup water

1. Coat the bottom and sides of a 1½-quart baking dish with cooking spray. Arrange the potato mixture in an even layer in the bottom of the dish. Top with half the cheddar in an even layer and top that with the bacon.

2. In a large bowl, whisk together the eggs, half-and-half, salt, and pepper. Pour over the potatoes, cheese, and bacon. Top with the remaining cheese.

3. Pour 1 cup of water into the inner pot and insert a trivet with handles. Place the baking dish on the trivet and place a square of foil over the dish.

4. Lock the lid into place. Select Pressure Cook or Manual; adjust the pressure to High and the time to 18 minutes.

5. When cooking is complete, quick-release the pressure. Remove the lid and lift out the baking dish and trivet. Remove the foil and let cool for 10 minutes to let the eggs set.

6. Scoop out onto plates and serve.

FREEZER FEAST TIP: Using frozen potatoes, assemble the casserole but omit the final layer of cheese. Cover with plastic wrap and then foil and freeze. To cook, thaw overnight in the refrigerator. Add the final layer of cheese and cook, adding 2 minutes to the cooking time.

Per Serving (brunch): Calories: 500; Fat: 36g; Protein: 30g; Total carbohydrates: 13g; Fiber: 1.5g; Sugar: 3g; Sodium: 929mg

Per Serving (breakfast): Calories: 333; Fat: 24g; Protein: 20g; Total carbohydrates: 9g; Fiber: 1g; Sugar: 2g; Sodium: 619mg

Huevos Rancheros with Refried Beans

5-INGREDIENT · 30-MINUTE · ONE-POT MEAL · VEGETARIAN

Serves 4

Prep time:
10 minutes

Pressure cook:
6 minutes

Release:
Quick

Total time:
30 minutes

Huevos rancheros, eggs cooked in a spicy sauce and served over tortillas, is a classic Mexican breakfast dish often accompanied by refried beans. In this recipe, I cook the two together, making the refried beans before simmering the eggs in sauce for a one-dish, filling breakfast.

4 small corn tortillas
Cooking spray
½ teaspoon kosher salt, divided
1 tablespoon vegetable oil or olive oil
2 (15-ounce) cans pinto beans, undrained

⅔ cup Restaurant-Style Salsa (page 145) or store-bought salsa, divided
4 large eggs
1 cup shredded Monterey Jack cheese (about 2 ounces)

1. Mist one side of each tortilla with cooking spray and sprinkle the tortillas on one side with salt (¼ teaspoon total). Stack the tortillas and wrap in aluminum foil. Set aside.

2. Pour the oil into the inner pot. Reserving the liquid, drain the beans. Add the beans, 2 tablespoons of the salsa, and ¼ cup of the reserved bean liquid (reserve the remainder). Stir to combine.

3. Place a tall trivet in the pot over the beans and place the wrapped tortillas on it. Lock the lid into place. Select Pressure Cook or Manual; adjust the pressure to High and the time to 4 minutes.

4. When cooking is complete, quick-release the pressure. Remove the trivet and tortillas. Cover the tortillas with a towel to keep warm and set aside.

5. Use a potato masher to mash the beans into a coarse paste, adding more bean liquid if necessary to get the right consistency.

6. Using the back of a large spoon, make 4 depressions in the beans. Carefully crack an egg into each depression and sprinkle with the remaining ¼ teaspoon of salt. Drizzle the remaining salsa over and around the eggs.

7. Lock the lid into place. Select Pressure Cook or Manual; adjust the pressure to High and the time to 1 minute.

8. When cooking is complete, quick-release the pressure. Remove the lid. The eggs should be barely set. Sprinkle the Monterey Jack over the eggs and beans. Replace the lid but don't lock it into place; let sit until the eggs finish cooking and the cheese melts.

9. Remove the lid. Place the tortillas on plates. Carefully scoop out a small spoonful of beans with an egg sitting on top, and place it on a tortilla. Repeat with the remaining eggs and tortillas. Spoon the remaining beans onto the plates next to the tortillas. Serve with more salsa, if desired.

   VARIATION: Try this dish with green enchilada sauce in place of the salsa.

Per Serving: Calories: 441; Fat: 23g; Protein: 24g; Total carbohydrates: 39g; Fiber: 8.5g; Sugar: 2g; Sodium: 810mg

Ham and Swiss Strata

5-INGREDIENT

Serves 4 for brunch, 6 for breakfast

Ham and Swiss cheese on rye bread is one of my favorite sandwich combinations. I developed this dish after I had some dental work that put me on soft foods for a few months. Craving my favorite, I turned it into a savory bread pudding. All the flavor, but easier to eat.

Prep time:
10 minutes

Pressure cook:
17 minutes

Release:
Quick

Cooling time:
10 minutes

Total time:
45 minutes

3 large eggs
¾ cup half-and-half or whole milk
½ teaspoon kosher salt
6 ounces stale rye bread, cut into ¾-inch cubes (about 4 cups)

Cooking spray
6 ounces ham, diced
2 cups shredded Gruyère or other Swiss-style cheese (about 4 ounces)
1 cup water

1. In a large bowl, whisk together the eggs, half-and-half, and salt. Add the bread cubes and gently stir to coat with the eggs. Let sit for a few minutes, then toss again. Most of the egg mixture should be absorbed.

2. Mist the bottom and sides of a 1½-quart baking dish with cooking spray. Transfer half the bread cubes to the dish in an even layer. Top with half the ham and half the Gruyère. Spoon over the remaining bread with any remaining egg mixture. Top with the remaining ham and finish with the remaining cheese.

3. Pour 1 cup of water into the inner pot and insert a trivet with handles. Place the baking dish on the trivet and place a square of foil over the dish.

4. Lock the lid into place. Select Pressure Cook or Manual; adjust the pressure to High and the time to 17 minutes.

5. When cooking is complete, quick-release the pressure. Remove the lid and lift out the baking dish and trivet. Remove the foil and let cool for 10 minutes to let the eggs set.

6. Scoop out onto plates and serve.

FLAVOR BOOST: While the strata is delicious as is, adding a tablespoon of Dijon mustard and a teaspoon of Worcestershire to the egg mixture gives it some extra depth and complexity.

Per Serving (brunch): Calories: 467; Fat: 31g; Protein: 26g; Total carbohydrates: 23g; Fiber: 2.5g; Sugar: 4g; Sodium: 862mg

Per Serving (breakfast): Calories: 311; Fat: 20g; Protein: 17g; Total carbohydrates: 15g; Fiber: 1.5g; Sugar: 2.5g; Sodium: 575mg

Smoked Salmon Mini-Quiches

5-INGREDIENT • 30-MINUTE

Serves 4

Though you can't make a traditional quiche in the Instant Pot, you can make a delicious crustless version. You might not get the crunch of the crust, but you do get a silky-smooth filling.

Prep time:
8 minutes

Steam:
7 minutes

Release:
Quick

Total time:
30 minutes

Cooking spray
2 ounces smoked salmon, flaked
2 ounces cream cheese, cut into ¼-inch pieces
4 large eggs

⅔ cup half-and-half
½ teaspoon kosher salt
¼ teaspoon ground white pepper
1 cup water

1. Mist four 1-cup custard cups or ramekins with cooking spray. Divide the smoked salmon and cream cheese bits between the cups.

2. In a medium bowl, whisk the eggs. Add the half-and-half, salt, and white pepper. Whisk until no streaks of egg remain. Divide the egg mixture between the cups.

3. Pour 1 cup of water into the inner pot and place a trivet inside. Place the cups on the trivet, stacking as necessary. Place a square of foil over the cups.

4. Lock the lid into place. Select Steam; adjust the pressure to High and the time to 7 minutes.

5. When cooking is complete, quick-release the pressure. Remove the lid and lift out the foil. Using tongs, remove the custard cups. The quiches should be just set; if the centers are still runny, return them to the Instant Pot and set the lid on for a few minutes.

6. Let cool for a few minutes before serving.

Per Serving: Calories: 212; Fat: 18g; Protein: 11g; Total carbohydrates: 3g; Fiber: 0g; Sugar: 2.5g; Sodium: 375mg

Nutty Maple Polenta

5-INGREDIENT • **30-MINUTE** • **DAIRY-FREE** • **ONE-POT MEAL**
QUICK PREP • **VEGETARIAN**

Serves 6

Prep time:
2 minutes

Sauté:
5 minutes

Pressure cook:
10 minutes

Release:
Quick

Total time:
25 minutes

If you've only had polenta with dinner, you'll be delighted to try it for breakfast. Quick and easy, this creamy vegan version makes a wonderful alternative to oatmeal.

3 cups water
2 cups unsweetened plant-based milk

1 cup polenta
½ cup pecan or walnut pieces
¼ cup maple syrup

1. Select Sauté and adjust the heat to Low. In the inner pot, whisk together the water, milk, and polenta. Continue to whisk frequently for 5 minutes, until the mixture reaches a simmer, then press Cancel.

2. Lock the lid into place. Select Pressure Cook or Manual; adjust the pressure to High and the time to 10 minutes.

3. When cooking is complete, quick-release the pressure. Remove the lid. Add the nuts and maple syrup and stir well to combine.

4. Serve immediately.

VARIATION: Turn this into a savory breakfast by omitting the maple syrup and nuts and adding sautéed fresh vegetables such as mushrooms, zucchini, spinach, chard, or kale. Top with fresh tomatoes or salsa and sprinkle with a bit of Parmesan cheese.

Per Serving: Calories: 212; Fat: 8g; Protein: 4g; Total carbohydrates: 32g; Fiber: 1g; Sugar: 8g; Sodium: 64mg

Spiced Apple French Toast Casserole

5-INGREDIENT · VEGETARIAN

Serves 6

Prep time:
10 minutes

Pressure cook:
17 minutes

Release:
Quick

Cooling time:
10 minutes

Total time:
40 minutes

Turning French toast into an Instant Pot casserole is the perfect way to make an impressive, but easy, breakfast for a crowd. Apple pie filling with a hint of spice is a delicious addition to the dish.

3 large eggs
¾ cup half-and-half or whole milk
Pinch kosher salt
6 ounces stale challah or similar bread, cut into ¾-inch cubes (about 4 cups)

1 (21-ounce) can apple pie filling
1 teaspoon ground cinnamon or apple pie spice
Cooking spray
1 cup water

1. In a large bowl, whisk together the eggs, half-and-half, and salt. Add the bread cubes and gently stir to coat with the eggs. Let sit for a few minutes, then toss again. Most of the egg mixture should be absorbed. Gently stir in the apple pie filling and cinnamon.

2. Mist a 1½-quart baking dish with cooking spray. Spoon the bread and apple mixture into the dish.

3. Pour 1 cup of water into the inner pot and place a trivet inside. Place the baking dish on the trivet and place a square of foil over the dish.

4. Lock the lid into place. Select Pressure Cook or Manual; adjust the pressure to High and the time to 17 minutes.

5. When cooking is complete, quick-release the pressure. Remove the lid and use the trivet handles to lift out the baking dish. Remove the foil and let cool for 10 minutes to let the eggs set.

6. Scoop out onto plates and serve.

Per Serving: Calories: 274; Fat: 9.5g; Protein: 7g; Total carbohydrates: 42g; Fiber: 1g; Sugar: 16g; Sodium: 262mg

Breakfast Blueberry Pudding Cakes

VEGETARIAN

Serves 4

Prep time:
10 minutes

Pressure cook:
8 minutes

Release:
Quick

Cooling time:
3 minutes

Total time:
35 minutes

These delightful breakfast treats combine the best of muffins and soft, creamy pudding—a sort of blueberry lava cake. The recipe includes a hint of cardamom, which is a wonderful accent to the berries, but if you don't have it, you can substitute cinnamon or just leave it out. They're tasty either way.

4 tablespoons (½ stick) unsalted butter, at room temperature
½ cup sugar
1 large egg
½ teaspoon vanilla extract
¾ cup self-rising flour

½ teaspoon ground cardamom (optional)
6 tablespoons whole milk
½ cup blueberries
Cooking spray
1 cup water

1. In a large bowl, with an electric mixer, beat together the butter and sugar until creamy and light colored, about 2 minutes. Beat in the egg and vanilla until well combined.

2. Add about half of the flour and the cardamom (if using) and mix on low speed. Add the milk and mix again. Add the remaining flour and mix. Gently stir in the blueberries.

3. Mist four 1-cup ramekins or custard cups with cooking spray. Divide the batter between the cups.

4. Pour 1 cup of water into the inner pot and place the trivet inside. Place the cups on the trivet, stacking as necessary. Place a piece of foil over the cups.

5. Lock the lid into place. Select Pressure Cook or Manual; adjust the pressure to High and the time to 8 minutes.

6. When cooking is complete, quick-release the pressure. Remove the lid and lift out the foil. Using tongs, remove the cups and let cool for 3 minutes.

7. Dig in while they're still warm!

VARIATION: For a more traditional blueberry muffin, simply bake them for an additional 2 minutes and let cool for 10 minutes. Run a small knife or offset spatula around the inside of the cups and invert the muffins onto a plate for serving.

Per Serving: Calories: 351; Fat: 17g; Protein: 5g; Total carbohydrates: 47g; Fiber: 1g; Sugar: 28g; Sodium: 309mg

Pumpkin-Gingerbread Muffins

DAIRY-FREE · VEGETARIAN

Serves 4

Prep time:
10 minutes

Pressure cook:
8 minutes

Release:
Quick

Cooling time:
5 minutes

Total time:
35 minutes

If you're in love with pumpkin spice, you'll fall for these tasty gingerbread muffins with their hint of pumpkin pie flavor. They're fast enough to make in the morning, but you can also make them ahead of time for an even easier breakfast.

3 tablespoons very hot water
¼ cup canned unsweetened pumpkin puree
2 tablespoons vegetable oil
¼ cup packed light brown sugar
¼ cup molasses
1 large egg

¾ cup all-purpose flour
¼ teaspoon baking powder
¼ teaspoon baking soda
¼ teaspoon fine salt
¾ teaspoon ground ginger
½ teaspoon ground cinnamon
Cooking spray
1 cup water

1. In a small bowl, use a hand mixer to combine the hot water, pumpkin puree, oil, brown sugar, molasses, and egg.

2. In a separate bowl, whisk together the flour, baking powder, baking soda, salt, ginger, and cinnamon. Add to the liquid mixture. Mix on medium speed until the ingredients are thoroughly combined with no lumps.

3. Mist the insides of four 1-cup custard cups or ramekins with cooking spray. Divide the batter between the cups.

4. Add 1 cup water to the inner pot and place the trivet inside. Place the custard cups on the trivet, stacking as necessary, and place a square of aluminum foil over the cups.

5. Lock the lid into place. Select Pressure Cook or Manual, adjust the pressure to High, and set the time to 8 minutes.

6. When cooking is complete, quick-release the pressure. Remove the lid and lift out the foil. Using tongs, remove the cups. Let them cool for at least 5 minutes.

7. Flip them out of the ramekins to serve.

   SUBSTITUTION TIP: If you can't find pumpkin puree, you can substitute applesauce. Everything else remains the same.

Per Serving: Calories: 305; Fat: 12g; Protein: 4g; Total carbohydrates: 48g; Fiber: 1g; Sugar: 29g; Sodium: 254mg

Vegetables and Sides

Potato and Snap Pea Salad

5-INGREDIENT • DAIRY-FREE • VEGETARIAN

Serves 6

Sugar snap peas make an unusual and surprisingly tasty addition to potato salad. A savory vinaigrette makes a nice change from the more typical mayonnaise-based dressing in this quick side dish.

Prep time:
10 minutes

Pressure cook:
4 minutes

Release:
Quick

Cooling time:
10 minutes

Total time:
35 minutes

1 cup water

1 ½ pounds Yukon Gold potatoes (4 or 5 medium), peeled and cut into 1-inch cubes

1 shallot, finely chopped

¼ cup apple cider vinegar

¼ cup olive oil

1 teaspoon Dijon mustard

½ teaspoon kosher salt

4 ounces sugar snap peas, halved lengthwise

1. Pour 1 cup of water into the inner pot and insert the trivet or a steamer basket. Add the potatoes.

2. Lock the lid in place. Select Pressure Cook or Manual; adjust the pressure to High and the time to 4 minutes.

3. While the potatoes cook, in a large bowl, whisk together the shallot, vinegar, oil, mustard, and salt. Set the dressing aside.

4. When cooking is complete, quick-release the pressure. Remove the lid and transfer the cooked potatoes to the bowl of dressing. Stir in the peas.

5. Cool for 10 minutes before serving, or serve chilled.

SUBSTITUTION TIP: If you can't find sugar snap peas, use fresh green beans.

Per Serving: Calories: 176; Fat: 9g; Protein: 3g; Total carbohydrates: 23g; Fiber: 2.5g; Sugar: 2g; Sodium: 57mg

Green Beans with Shallots and Bacon

5-INGREDIENT · 30-MINUTE · DAIRY-FREE

Serves 6

Prep time:
10 minutes

Sauté:
7 minutes

Pressure cook:
2 minutes

Release:
Quick

Total time:
30 minutes

Green beans simmered with bacon are a classic side dish, one that traditionally takes an hour or more on the stovetop. This version keeps the beans crisp and fresh-tasting, while the bacon and shallots add texture and plenty of flavor.

1 cup water
1 pound green beans, trimmed
2 bacon slices, chopped

2 shallots, chopped
½ teaspoon kosher salt

1. Pour 1 cup water into the inner pot and insert a steamer basket or trivet. Place the green beans in the steamer or on the trivet.

2. Lock the lid into place. Select Pressure Cook or Manual; adjust the pressure to High and the time to 2 minutes.

3. When cooking is complete, quick-release the pressure. Remove the lid. Remove the steamer or trivet and set the beans aside.

4. Pour the water out of the inner pot, dry it, and return it to the base. Select Sauté and adjust the heat to Medium. Add the bacon, shallots, and ¼ teaspoon of salt. Sauté for 5 to 7 minutes, until the bacon crisps and the shallots are browned.

5. Add the green beans to the bacon-shallot mixture and sprinkle with the remaining ¼ teaspoon of salt. Toss gently and serve hot.

VARIATION: For a sweeter dish, add 1 tablespoon of brown sugar when adding the beans to the shallots and bacon.

Per Serving: Calories: 72; Fat: 4g; Protein: 3g; Total carbohydrates: 8g; Fiber: 2.5g; Sugar: 3.5g; Sodium: 161mg

Warm Broccoli Salad with Pine Nuts

5-INGREDIENT · 30-MINUTE · DAIRY-FREE · QUICK PREP · VEGETARIAN

Serves 4

Prep time:
5 minutes

Sauté:
4 minutes

Steam:
0 minutes

Release:
Quick

Total time:
18 minutes

If your experience with broccoli is soggy, overcooked florets coated with cheese sauce, you'll be surprised at how this versatile vegetable can shine when lightly steamed and tossed with a tangy dressing. Crunchy pine nuts are the perfect accent to this delicious salad.

1 pound broccoli florets
1 cup water
2 tablespoons olive oil, divided
½ teaspoon kosher salt
1 tablespoon balsamic vinegar

¼ teaspoon freshly ground black pepper
2 tablespoons toasted pine nuts

1. Place the broccoli florets in a steamer basket. Add 1 cup of water to the inner pot and place the steamer basket inside.

2. Lock the lid into place. Select Steam; adjust the pressure to High and the time to 0 minutes. (Steaming them for 0 minutes might seem strange, but by the time the pot comes to pressure, they're done!)

3. When cooking is complete, quick-release the pressure. Remove the lid and lift out the broccoli.

4. Pour the water out of the inner pot, dry it, and return it to the base. Select Sauté and adjust the heat to High. Add 1 tablespoon of oil and heat until it shimmers. Add the broccoli and salt and cook, stirring, for 1 to 2 minutes, until the broccoli browns in spots.

5. Transfer the broccoli to a large bowl and drizzle with the remaining 1 tablespoon of oil and the vinegar. Sprinkle with the pepper and toss to coat the broccoli. Top with the pine nuts.

VARIATION: Replace the broccoli with 1-inch pieces of asparagus. Cook time remains the same.

Per Serving: Calories: 123; Fat: 10g; Protein: 4g; Total carbohydrates: 7g; Fiber: 2.5g; Sugar: 2.5g; Sodium: 172mg

Cheesy Smashed Red Potatoes

5-INGREDIENT · 30-MINUTE · VEGETARIAN

Serves 4

Prep time:
12 minutes

Steam:
4 minutes

Release:
Quick

Total time:
25 minutes

Red potatoes are not really suitable for mashing—they can get gluey quickly. But lightly crushed with cream and cheese, they make an easy, tasty rustic accompaniment to grilled or roasted meats or poultry.

1½ pounds red potatoes, cut into 1-inch chunks

1 cup water

½ teaspoon kosher salt, or more to taste

¼ teaspoon freshly ground black pepper (several grinds)

½ cup heavy cream, or more to taste

1 cup shredded sharp cheddar cheese

2 scallions, chopped

1. Place the potatoes in a steamer basket. Pour 1 cup of water into the inner pot and place the steamer basket inside.

2. Lock the lid into place. Select Steam; adjust the pressure to High and the time to 4 minutes.

3. When cooking is complete, quick-release the pressure. Remove the lid and remove the steamer basket from the pot.

4. Pour the water out of the inner pot, dry it, and return it to the base. Return the potatoes to the pot and add the salt, pepper, and cream. Use a potato masher to lightly crush the potatoes into the cream, then stir in the cheddar. The potatoes should be chunky—too much mashing can make them gluey. Let sit for a few minutes until the cheese is melted, then stir in the scallions.

5. Adjust the seasoning and serve.

   VARIATION: Try these with Gruyère or Emmenthal cheese instead of the cheddar.

Per Serving: Calories: 338; Fat: 20g; Protein: 11g; Total carbohydrates: 29g; Fiber: 3g; Sugar: 3.5g; Sodium: 364mg

Curried Cauliflower and Peas

5-INGREDIENT • 30-MINUTE • DAIRY-FREE • QUICK PREP • VEGETARIAN

Serves 4

Prep time:
5 minutes

Pressure cook:
1 minute

Release:
Quick

Total time:
20 minutes

I'm not ordinarily a big fan of cauliflower, but I used to get a fabulous vegetable curry filled with cauliflower and peas at a neighborhood Indian restaurant. My take on it is not authentic, but it makes an easy, unusual side dish.

1 pound cauliflower florets

1 cup canned full-fat coconut milk

1½ teaspoons Indian curry paste, or more to taste

½ teaspoon curry powder

¼ teaspoon kosher salt

1 cup frozen green peas, thawed

1. Place the cauliflower in the inner pot. Add the coconut milk, curry paste, curry powder, and salt and stir gently to distribute the spices.

2. Lock the lid into place. Select Pressure Cook or Manual; adjust the pressure to High and the time to 1 minute.

3. When cooking is complete, quick-release the pressure. Remove the lid, stir in the peas, and let sit to heat through.

4. Adjust the seasoning and serve.

    SUBSTITUTION TIP: Several types of Indian curry pastes are available at most large grocery stores, some hotter than others. If you can't find curry paste, omit it and increase the curry powder to 1½ teaspoons and the salt to ½ teaspoon.

Per Serving: Calories: 80; Fat: 2g; Protein: 4g; Total carbohydrates: 13g; Fiber: 4g; Sugar: 5g; Sodium: 175mg

Mashed Chipotle Sweet Potatoes

5-INGREDIENT · 30-MINUTE · VEGETARIAN

Serves 6

Prep time:
10 minutes

Pressure cook:
9 minutes

Release:
Quick

Total time:
30 minutes

Sweet potatoes cook quickly under pressure, so they make a fast and easy weeknight side dish. As a bonus, after cooking the skins slip right off, so there's virtually no work before they go into the Instant Pot. The smoky heat of chipotle chiles is a wonderful accent to the sweet, earthy flavor of sweet potatoes.

1½ pounds sweet potatoes (3 small or 2 large)
1 cup water
3 tablespoons unsalted butter
⅓ cup heavy cream, or more if needed

½ teaspoon kosher salt
1½ teaspoons minced chipotle peppers in adobo sauce, or more to taste

1. Halve the sweet potatoes lengthwise. If they are very large, cut the halves in half.

2. Pour 1 cup of water into the inner pot and place the trivet inside. Place the sweet potato pieces on the trivet cut-side down in a single layer as much as possible. If they won't fit in one layer, stack them so that the steam can circulate around all the pieces.

3. Lock the lid into place. Select Pressure Cook or Manual; adjust the pressure to High and the time to 9 minutes.

4. When cooking is complete, quick-release the pressure. Remove the lid and lift the trivet and sweet potatoes out of the pot.

5. Pour the water out of the inner pot, dry it, and return it to the base.

6. Slip the skins from the sweet potatoes and return them to the pot. Add the butter, cream, salt, and chipotles and mash to a smooth puree with a potato masher, adding more cream as necessary.

VARIATION: Instead of the chipotle, mix the sweet potatoes with minced fresh rosemary and grated Parmesan cheese.

Per Serving: Calories: 115; Fat: 8.5g; Protein: 3g; Total carbohydrates: 8g; Fiber: 3g; Sugar: 2.5g; Sodium: 114mg

Honey Mustard–Glazed Brussels Sprouts

5-INGREDIENT · 30-MINUTE · VEGETARIAN

Serves 4

Prep time:
6 minutes

Sauté:
5 minutes

Pressure cook:
1 minute

Release:
Quick

Total time:
25 minutes

Whenever fall rolls around, I always keep an eye out for Brussels sprouts. Their flavor takes well to assertive seasonings like the mustard in this dish, while the honey tempers their slight bitterness.

1 pound Brussels sprouts, trimmed and halved
1 cup water
½ teaspoon kosher salt
1 tablespoon unsalted butter

1 teaspoon minced garlic
1 tablespoon Dijon mustard
1 tablespoon honey
⅛ teaspoon freshly ground black pepper

1. Place the Brussels sprouts in a steaming basket. Pour 1 cup water into the inner pot and place the steaming basket inside.

2. Lock the lid into place. Select Steam; adjust the pressure to High and the time to 1 minute.

3. When cooking is complete, quick-release the pressure. Remove the lid, lift out the Brussels sprouts, and sprinkle with the salt.

4. Pour the water out of the inner pot, dry it, and return it to the base. Select Sauté and adjust the heat to Medium. Add the butter. When it's melted, add the garlic and cook, stirring, for 1 minute. Add the mustard, honey, and pepper and stir to dissolve the honey. Add the sprouts and stir to coat with sauce and rewarm, about 2 minutes.

   SUBSTITUTION TIP: For a dairy-free dish, replace the butter with olive oil.

Per Serving: Calories: 94; Fat: 3g; Protein: 4g; Total carbohydrates: 14g; Fiber: 4.5g; Sugar: 6.5g; Sodium: 259mg

Cumin-Scented Buttered Carrots

5-INGREDIENT • 30-MINUTE • QUICK PREP • VEGETARIAN

Serves 4

Prep time:
3 minutes

Sauté:
3 minutes

Pressure cook:
3 minutes

Release:
Quick

Total time:
20 minutes

I first had carrots flavored with cumin in a Turkish cooking class I attended years ago, and ever since then it's been one of my favorite ways to serve them. The pungent notes of the cumin complement the sweetness of the carrots and also highlight their earthy character.

2 tablespoons unsalted butter
1 teaspoon cumin seed
1 teaspoon kosher salt

1 pound baby carrots
¼ cup water

1. Select Sauté and adjust the heat to High. Add the butter and heat until foaming. Add the cumin and cook, stirring, for about 30 seconds, or until fragrant. Press Cancel.

2. Add the carrots, salt, and water to the pot.

3. Lock the lid into place. Select Pressure Cook or Manual; adjust the pressure to High and the time to 3 minutes.

4. When cooking is complete, quick-release the pressure.

5. Remove the lid. Select Sauté and adjust the heat to High. Bring the liquid to a boil and cook, stirring, until the water has evaporated and the cumin butter coats the carrots.

6. Serve hot.

SUBSTITUTION TIP: If you prefer, use 1 pound of regular carrots, peeled, trimmed, and cut into 1-inch lengths. Cut in half lengthwise if the carrots are very thick.

Per Serving: Calories: 93; Fat: 6g; Protein: 1g; Total carbohydrates: 10g; Fiber: 3.5g; Sugar: 5.5g; Sodium: 370mg

Spicy Corn and Black Beans

5-INGREDIENT • 30-MINUTE • DAIRY-FREE • QUICK PREP • VEGETARIAN

Serves 4

Prep time:
5 minutes

Pressure cook:
4 minutes

Release:
Quick

Total time:
25 minutes

Black beans are a great match for the sweetness of corn and bell peppers. This hearty recipe gives them a Southwestern flavor with salsa and chili powder.

1 (15.5-ounce) can black beans, drained and rinsed
1½ cups frozen corn, thawed
½ cup prechopped onion and bell pepper blend
¼ cup Restaurant-Style Salsa (page 145) or store-bought salsa
2 tablespoons water
1 tablespoon chili powder
½ teaspoon kosher salt

1. Pour the beans into the inner pot. Add the corn, onions and peppers, salsa, water, chili powder, and salt and stir to combine.

2. Lock the lid into place. Select Pressure Cook or Manual; adjust the pressure to High and the time to 4 minutes.

3. When cooking is complete, quick-release the pressure. Stir the contents and adjust the seasoning before serving.

   VARIATION: Though this flavorful mixture is a great side dish for any Southwestern entrée, it also makes a delicious filling for tacos or burritos. Top with shredded Monterey Jack cheese, salsa, and avocado for an easy taco night.

Per Serving: Calories: 145; Fat: 0.5g; Protein: 8g; Total carbohydrates: 29g; Fiber: 8.5g; Sugar: 2g; Sodium: 581mg

Soups and Stews

Broccoli-Cheddar Soup

ONE-POT MEAL • VEGETARIAN

Serves 6

Prep time:
10 minutes

Sauté:
5 minutes

Pressure cook:
3 minutes

Release:
Natural
(10 minutes),
then quick

Total time:
40 minutes

For a great way to get your kids to eat their vegetables, nothing beats broccoli-cheddar soup. It's creamy and cheesy but still relatively healthy— what more can you ask for?

1 tablespoon extra-virgin olive oil

1 cup chopped yellow onion

2 teaspoons minced garlic

3 cups Vegetable Broth (page 148) or store-bought low-sodium vegetable broth

1 pound fresh or thawed frozen broccoli florets (about 3½ cups)

3 cups shredded cheddar cheese

2 cups low-fat (1%) milk

1. Select Sauté and adjust the heat to Medium. Add the olive oil to the inner pot and heat until shimmering or the display reads "Hot." Add the onion and garlic and sauté for about 2 minutes.

2. Press Cancel and add the broth. Using a wooden spoon, scrape up any browned bits stuck to the bottom of the pot. Add the broccoli to the pot.

3. Lock the lid into place. Select Pressure Cook or Manual; set the pressure to High and the time to 3 minutes.

4. When cooking is complete, let the pressure release naturally for 10 minutes, then quick-release any remaining pressure.

5. Remove the lid. Select Sauté and adjust the heat to Low. Stir in the cheddar until melted and combined. Stir in the milk.

6. Let the soup come to a gentle simmer, then taste and adjust the seasoning. Serve immediately.

Per Serving: Calories: 333; Fat: 24g; Protein: 18g; Total carbohydrates: 13g; Fiber: 2g; Sugar: 7g; Sodium: 466mg

Butternut Squash and Corn Chowder with Bacon

ONE-POT MEAL

Serves 4

Prep time:
8 minutes

Sauté:
5 minutes

Pressure cook:
8 minutes

Release:
Quick

Total time:
35 minutes

Whichever produce manager first thought of selling peeled, cubed butternut squash deserves a medal. Now, instead of spending time splitting, peeling, seeding, and chopping squash, you can get right to making this delicious soup, which will be ready almost before you know it.

1 tablespoon unsalted butter
2 bacon slices, chopped
½ cup chopped onion
4 cups Vegetable Broth (page 148) or store-bought low-sodium vegetable broth

2 (12-ounce) bags frozen corn kernels (no need to thaw)
4 cups cubed butternut squash
½ teaspoon dried thyme
1 teaspoon dried chives

1. Select Sauté and adjust the heat to Medium. Add the butter, bacon, and onion to the pot and sauté for 5 minutes, or until the bacon is cooked and the onions are translucent.

2. Add the vegetable broth, corn, butternut squash, thyme, and chives to the pot.

3. Lock the lid into place. Select Pressure Cook or Manual; adjust the pressure to High and the time to 8 minutes.

4. When cooking is complete, quick-release the pressure. Remove the lid. Use an immersion blender to puree the soup, leaving a bit of texture.

5. Adjust the seasoning and serve.

   SUBSTITUTION TIP: To make this soup vegan, replace the butter with olive oil and omit the bacon.

Per Serving: Calories: 339; Fat: 13g; Protein: 9g; Total carbohydrates: 54g; Fiber: 6.5g; Sugar: 9g; Sodium: 184mg

Chorizo Chili

30-MINUTE • DAIRY-FREE • ONE-POT MEAL • QUICK PREP

Serves 4

Prep time:
5 minutes

Sauté:
5 minutes

Pressure cook:
6 minutes

Release:
Quick

Total time:
30 minutes

Starting with Mexican chorizo gives tons of flavor to this chili with fewer ingredients than most recipes. (Don't confuse it with Spanish chorizo, which is a cured, dry sausage.) I use Johnsonville brand chorizo, which is moderately spicy without a lot of fat. If you use a brand with more fat, you may want to drain some of it after the chorizo browns.

Cooking spray

1 pound fresh Mexican chorizo, casings removed if necessary

½ cup chopped onion

2 teaspoons minced garlic

1 (14.5-ounce) can fire-roasted diced tomatoes

2 (15-ounce) cans pinto beans, drained

2 tablespoons chili powder, or more to taste

¼ teaspoon kosher salt

¼ cup Chicken Stock (page 147) or store-bought low-sodium chicken stock, optional

1 small avocado, chopped, or ½ cup prepared guacamole, for garnish (optional)

1. Select Sauté and adjust the heat to High. Mist the bottom of the inner pot with a light coat of cooking spray. Heat until the display reads "Hot" and add the chorizo, breaking it up with a spoon. Cook for 1 to 2 minutes, just until it starts to brown (it doesn't need to cook completely). Add the onion and stir, cooking for another minute. Stir in the garlic. Press Cancel.

2. Add the tomatoes and stir, scraping up any browned food on the bottom of the pot. Add the beans, chili powder, and salt and stir to combine.

3. Lock the lid into place. Select Pressure Cook or Manual; adjust the pressure to High and the time to 6 minutes.

Continued >>

4. When cooking is complete, quick-release the pressure. Remove the lid and let sit for a minute. Use a paper towel to blot any fat on the top of the chili. If you prefer a looser consistency, stir in the chicken stock.

5. If desired, serve garnished with avocado or guacamole.

FLAVOR BOOST: For a kid-friendly favorite, serve the chili as "Frito Pie" by spooning it over a big handful of corn chips and topping with grated cheese, sour cream, and chopped onions.

Per Serving: Calories: 657; Fat: 31g; Protein: 35g; Total carbohydrates: 54g; Fiber: 15g; Sugar: 6g; Sodium: 1,634mg

Garlic Soup with Eggs and Spinach

DAIRY-FREE • ONE-POT MEAL • VEGETARIAN

Serves 4

Prep time:
10 minutes

Sauté:
7 minutes

Pressure cook:
6 minutes

Release:
Natural
(8 minutes),
then quick

Total time:
45 minutes

Versions of garlic soup with eggs are common throughout Spain and southern France. This recipe calls for a lot of garlic, but don't be intimidated: As it cooks, it mellows dramatically, giving a subtle, sweet flavor to the soup. And don't worry about peeling all those cloves—you can buy a bag of already peeled garlic.

40 peeled garlic cloves
   (4 ounces)
1 cup chopped onion
½ cup dry white wine
1 medium russet potato (about
   12 ounces), peeled and cut
   into 1-inch pieces

4 cups Vegetable Broth
   (page 148) or store-bought
   low-sodium vegetable broth
1 teaspoon dried thyme
¼ teaspoon ground white
   pepper
6 ounces baby spinach
4 large eggs

1. Select Sauté and adjust the heat to Medium. Add the garlic, onion, and wine and bring to a simmer. Cook for 2 to 3 minutes, until the wine has reduced by about one-third and some of the alcohol has evaporated. Press Cancel.

2. Add the potato, broth, thyme, and white pepper and stir to combine.

3. Lock the lid into place. Select Pressure Cook or Manual; adjust the pressure to High and the time to 6 minutes.

4. When cooking is complete, let the pressure release naturally for 8 minutes, then quick-release any remaining pressure. Remove the lid.

Continued >>

5. Using an immersion blender, puree the soup. Select Sauté and adjust the heat to Low. Stir in the spinach. When it has wilted and the soup is at a bare simmer, carefully crack the eggs into the soup. You may find it easier to crack the eggs into ramekins and then tip them into the soup. Cook for 3 to 4 minutes, until they are set with runny yolks.

6. To serve, carefully spoon an egg into each of four bowls and ladle the soup over.

FLAVOR BOOST: If you're not vegetarian, a sprinkle of chopped cooked bacon makes a great addition to the soup.

Per Serving: Calories: 261; Fat: 8.5g; Protein: 11g; Total carbohydrates: 31g; Fiber: 3.5g; Sugar: 3.5g; Sodium: 189mg

Stuffed Cabbage Soup

30-MINUTE • DAIRY-FREE • ONE-POT MEAL • QUICK PREP

Serves 4

Prep time:
5 minutes

Sauté:
5 minutes

Pressure cook:
4 minutes

Release:
Natural
(6 minutes),
then quick

Total time:
30 minutes

I love cabbage rolls, but I have a confession to make: Every time I've thought about making them, I've given up before even starting—they're so time-consuming! However, it turns out you can get the flavors of cabbage rolls in an easy, quick soup. Using chopped vegetables from the produce section makes it even faster and easier.

Cooking spray
1 pound ground beef (85% to 90% lean)
1 cup chopped onion
2 garlic cloves, minced
2 (14.5-ounce) cans diced tomatoes
4 cups low-sodium beef broth
1 teaspoon kosher salt, divided
½ cup long-grain white rice

4 cups sliced green cabbage
½ cup chopped carrots
1 bay leaf
1 teaspoon dried thyme
2 teaspoons light brown sugar
1 teaspoon cider vinegar or wine vinegar
¼ teaspoon freshly ground black pepper

1. Select Sauté and adjust the heat to High. Mist the bottom of the inner pot with a light coating of cooking spray. Heat until the display reads "Hot" and add the ground beef, breaking it up with a spoon. Cook for 1 to 2 minutes, just until it starts to brown (it doesn't need to cook completely). Add the onion and stir, cooking for another minute. Stir in the garlic. Press Cancel.

2. Add the tomatoes, broth, salt, rice, cabbage, carrots, bay leaf, and thyme and stir to combine.

3. Lock the lid into place. Select Pressure Cook or Manual; adjust the pressure to High and the time to 4 minutes.

4. When cooking is complete, let the pressure release naturally for 6 minutes, then quick-release any remaining pressure.

5. Remove the lid and stir in the brown sugar, vinegar, and pepper. Adjust the seasoning and serve.

   SUBSTITUTION TIP: If you can't find sliced cabbage in the produce section, look for coleslaw mix. Just avoid "angel-hair" slaw mixes, which cook too quickly.

Per Serving: Calories: 480; Fat: 21g; Protein: 30g; Total carbohydrates: 43g; Fiber: 7g; Sugar: 13g; Sodium: 845mg

Creamy Turkey and Wild Rice Soup

ONE-POT MEAL • QUICK PREP

Serves 4

Prep time:
5 minutes

Sauté:
5 minutes

Pressure cook:
20 minutes

Release:
Natural
(10 minutes),
then quick

Total time:
1 hour

Who says turkey is only for Thanksgiving? This delicious soup combines turkey thigh meat with wild rice and vegetables for a fast, filling weeknight meal. It'll change your mind about that holiday bird.

4 cups Chicken Stock (page 147) or store-bought low-sodium chicken stock
¾ cup wild rice
½ teaspoon kosher salt
2 medium bone-in turkey thighs, skinned
1 cup chopped onion
1 or 2 sprigs fresh thyme or 1 teaspoon dried thyme

½ teaspoon dried sage
1 bay leaf
1 teaspoon Worcestershire sauce
1½ cups frozen mixed vegetables, thawed
¼ teaspoon freshly ground black pepper
½ cup heavy cream

1. Pour the chicken stock into the inner pot. Stir in the wild rice and salt. Add the turkey thighs, onion, thyme, sage, bay leaf, and Worcestershire sauce.

2. Lock the lid into place. Select Pressure Cook or Manual; adjust the pressure to High and the time to 20 minutes.

3. When cooking is complete, let the pressure release naturally for 10 minutes, then quick-release any remaining pressure.

4. Remove the lid. Use tongs to remove the turkey thighs to a cutting board. Discard the thyme sprigs and bay leaf.

5. Add the mixed vegetables, black pepper, and cream to the inner pot. Select Sauté and adjust the heat to Low. Bring to a simmer and let cook until the vegetables are cooked through, about 5 minutes.

6. While the soup simmers, remove the turkey meat from the bones and chop it. Return it to the soup to warm through.

7. Adjust the seasonings and serve.

   VARIATION: Use one fresh turkey thigh and one smoked turkey thigh. Omit the cream.

   EVEN EASIER: After Thanksgiving, use leftover shredded turkey in the soup. Add it at the very end just to heat through.

Per Serving: Calories: 667; Fat: 20g; Protein: 84g; Total carbohydrates: 39g; Fiber: 4g; Sugar: 7.5g; Sodium: 782mg

Artichoke-Spinach Soup

30-MINUTE • ONE-POT MEAL

Serves 4

Prep time:
6 minutes

Sauté:
5 minutes

Pressure cook:
4 minutes

Release:
Natural
(5 minutes),
then quick

Total time:
30 minutes

It's hardly a secret how well spinach and artichokes go together—just think of all those dip recipes out there. Unlike lots of those dips, this easy soup lets the vegetables shine, with just a hint of cream and Parmesan to round out the flavors.

1 (12-ounce) bag frozen
   artichoke hearts, thawed
1 cup chopped onion
2 teaspoons minced garlic
½ teaspoon kosher salt

4 cups Vegetable Broth
   (page 148) or store-bought
   low-sodium vegetable broth
12 ounces fresh spinach
⅓ cup heavy cream
½ cup grated Parmesan cheese

1. In the inner pot, combine the artichoke hearts, onion, garlic, salt, and broth.

2. Lock the lid into place. Select Pressure Cook or Manual; adjust the pressure to High and the time to 4 minutes.

3. When cooking is complete, let the pressure release naturally for 5 minutes, then quick-release any remaining pressure. Remove the lid.

4. Select Sauté and adjust the heat to Low. Add the spinach and bring to a simmer, cooking until the spinach is wilted, about 2 minutes.

5. Use an immersion blender to blend to a coarse puree, then stir in the cream and Parmesan. Heat through, then adjust the seasoning and serve.

INGREDIENT TIP: Buy vegetarian Parmesan if you're strictly vegetarian.

Per Serving: Calories: 210; Fat: 13g; Protein: 8g; Total carbohydrates: 15g; Fiber: 8.5g; Sugar: 3g; Sodium: 397mg

Thai-Inspired Chicken Soup

30-MINUTE • DAIRY-FREE • ONE-POT MEAL • QUICK PREP

Serves 4

Prep time:
5 minutes

Pressure cook:
4 minutes

Release:
Natural
(4 minutes),
then quick

Total time:
30 minutes

One of my favorite dishes to order at Thai restaurants is tom kha gai, *a spicy, coconut-based chicken soup flavored with galangal, lemongrass, and makrut lime leaves. Because those ingredients are difficult to find, I've come up with this soup, which is reminiscent of the original.*

3 cups Chicken Stock (page 147) or store-bought low-sodium chicken stock
1 (14-ounce) can full-fat coconut milk
2 teaspoons minced garlic
1 teaspoon minced fresh ginger
2 teaspoons red Thai curry paste
12 ounces chicken tenders
8 ounces sliced white mushrooms

½ cup sliced onion
1 teaspoon fish sauce, or more to taste
1 tablespoon fresh lime juice, or more to taste
1 teaspoon sugar, or more to taste
2 scallions, thinly sliced, for garnish
¼ cup coarsely chopped fresh cilantro, for garnish

1. Pour the chicken stock and coconut milk into the inner pot. Stir in the garlic, ginger and curry paste. Add the chicken, mushrooms, and onion.

2. Lock the lid into place. Select Pressure Cook or Manual; adjust the pressure to High and the time to 4 minutes.

3. When cooking is complete, let the pressure release naturally for 4 minutes, then quick-release any remaining pressure.

4. Remove the lid and stir in the fish sauce, lime juice, and sugar. Taste and adjust the seasoning.

5. Serve garnished with the scallions and cilantro.

Per Serving: Calories: 346; Fat: 24g; Protein: 26g; Total carbohydrates: 10g; Fiber: 2.5g; Sugar: 4g; Sodium: 479mg

Beef and Potato Stew

DAIRY-FREE • ONE-POT MEAL • QUICK PREP

Serves 4

Prep time:
5 minutes

Sauté:
10 minutes

Pressure cook:
26 minutes

Release:
Quick

Total time:
55 minutes

When it comes to comfort food, there's nothing quite like a classic beef stew. Though this recipe is a bit time-consuming, it takes only a small fraction of the time of a traditional stew on the stovetop. In under an hour, you can have a satisfying and warming meal on the table.

1½ pounds petit tenders or mock tenders (beef shoulder)

½ teaspoon kosher salt, plus more to taste

2 tablespoons vegetable oil

1 cup dark beer (porter or stout)

1 (10.5-ounce) can condensed beef consommé

2 teaspoons Worcestershire sauce

1 small onion, peeled and halved

1 pound red potatoes, quartered

4 ounces baby carrots, halved

1 cup frozen pearl onions, thawed

1 cup frozen peas, thawed

¼ teaspoon freshly ground black pepper

1 tablespoon Wondra flour (optional)

1. Sprinkle the beef with ½ teaspoon salt.

2. Select Sauté and adjust the heat to High. Add the oil to the inner pot and heat until shimmering or the display reads "Hot." Add the beef and sear without moving for 2 to 3 minutes, until dark brown. Turn and brown the other side. Remove the beef to a rack or cutting board and set aside to cool slightly.

3. Add the beer to the pot and stir, scraping the bottom of the pan to dissolve the browned bits. Bring to a boil and cook for 1 to 2 minutes, until the beer has reduced by about one-third.

4. While the beer reduces, cut the beef into pieces about 1½ inches on a side.

5. When the beer has reduced, return the beef to the pot. Add the consommé, Worcestershire sauce, and onion halves.

6. Lock the lid in place. Select Pressure Cook or Manual; adjust the pressure to High and the time to 22 minutes.

7. When cooking is complete, quick-release the pressure. Remove the lid and discard the onion halves. Add the potatoes, carrots, and pearl onions.

8. Lock the lid in place. Select Pressure Cook or Manual; adjust the pressure to High and the time to 4 minutes.

9. After cooking is complete, quick-release the pressure. Remove the lid and stir in the peas to warm through. Season with the black pepper and additional salt, if necessary.

10. For a thicker sauce, whisk the Wondra with 1 tablespoon water and stir into the stew. Select Sauté and adjust the heat to Low. Bring to a simmer and let cook until thickened.

SUBSTITUTION TIP: I like to use undiluted consommé for an extra beefy flavor, but feel free to substitute beef stock or broth instead. You'll probably want to add salt, though, because the consommé is saltier than most broths.

Per Serving: Calories: 475; Fat: 19g; Protein: 42g; Total carbohydrates: 32g; Fiber: 5g; Sugar: 7g; Sodium: 593mg

Mexican-Inspired Shrimp Soup

30-MINUTE • DAIRY-FREE • ONE-POT MEAL

Serves 4

Prep time:
6 minutes

Sauté:
5 minutes

Pressure cook:
3 minutes

Release:
Natural
(3 minutes),
then quick

Total time:
30 minutes

Starting this soup by browning salsa might seem odd, but it mimics a typical Mexican technique of charring vegetables and pureeing as a base for many soups, stews, and sauces. Depending on the salsa you use, you may want to add the optional seasonings. I use Frontera brand Double Roasted Salsa, which provides a lot of flavor and a medium heat level.

1 tablespoon olive oil

1½ cups tomato-based salsa

4 ounces baby carrots, quartered

1 large Yukon Gold potato (about 8 ounces), peeled and cut into ½-inch chunks

4 cups seafood stock

1 pound peeled and deveined medium shrimp

1 teaspoon ground cumin (optional)

½ teaspoon cayenne pepper (optional)

2 teaspoons chili powder (optional)

1. Select Sauté and adjust the heat to High. Add the oil to the inner pot and heat until shimmering or the display reads "Hot." Add the salsa and cook until the liquid has reduced and the salsa is browning in spots, 2 to 3 minutes. Press Cancel.

2. Add the carrots, potato, and stock, scraping to get up any browned bits from the bottom of the pot.

3. Lock the lid into place. Select Pressure Cook or Manual; adjust the pressure to High and the time to 3 minutes.

4. When cooking is complete, let the pressure release naturally for 3 minutes, then quick-release any remaining pressure.

5. Remove the lid. Add the shrimp and let sit in the heat for 2 to 3 minutes, until opaque and cooked through.

6. Stir in the cumin, cayenne, and chili powder (if using) and serve.

SUBSTITUTION TIP: If you can't find seafood stock in your grocery store, there are several good stock bases available. Penzey's carries a line of stock bases, and More Than Gourmet and Better Than Bouillon also make a seafood stock base. These all contain salt, so keep that in mind when seasoning.

Per Serving: Calories: 202; Fat: 4g; Protein: 25g; Total carbohydrates: 17g; Fiber: 3g; Sugar: 4g; Sodium: 1,365mg

5

Vegetarian Mains

Green Pea and Parmesan Risotto

ONE-POT MEAL • VEGETARIAN

Serves 6

Prep time:
10 minutes

Sauté:
5 minutes

Pressure cook:
5 minutes

Release:
Natural
(5 minutes),
then quick

Total time:
35 minutes

The Instant Pot is a game changer when it comes to risotto. What usually takes an hour or more, with lots of standing and stirring, is done in half the time with almost no work. You won't believe risotto can be this easy!

2 tablespoons extra-virgin
   olive oil
1 cup chopped yellow onion
2 teaspoons minced garlic
4 cups Vegetable Broth
   (page 148) or store-bought
   low-sodium vegetable broth

2 cups arborio rice
1 (16-ounce) bag frozen
   green peas
1 cup grated Parmesan cheese

1. Select Sauté and adjust the heat to Medium. Add the olive oil to the inner pot. Once the oil is hot, add the onion and garlic and cook for 3 minutes or until they start to soften.

2. Press Cancel and pour in the broth. Using a wooden spoon, scrape up any browned bits stuck to the bottom of the pot. Add the rice and peas and stir to combine.

3. Lock the lid into place. Select Pressure Cook or Manual; set the pressure to High and the time to 5 minutes.

4. When cooking is complete, let the pressure release naturally for 5 minutes, then quick-release any remaining pressure.

5. Remove the lid and stir in the Parmesan.

6. Serve immediately.

   INGREDIENT TIP: Buy vegetarian Parmesan if you're strictly vegetarian.

Per Serving: Calories: 412; Fat: 11g; Protein: 13g; Total carbohydrates: 66g; Fiber: 6.5g; Sugar: 5g; Sodium: 345mg

Creamy Spaghetti Squash with Spinach, Olives, and Roasted Red Peppers

30-MINUTE • DAIRY-FREE • ONE-POT MEAL • VEGETARIAN

Serves 4

Prep time:
10 minutes

Pressure cook:
8 minutes

Release:
Quick

Total time:
30 minutes

If you're not familiar with spaghetti squash, it can be surprising and fun to see the dense, sturdy vegetable transform into thin, spaghetti-like strands. It makes a great vegan dinner when combined with spinach, olives, and roasted red peppers.

1 cup water
1 (3- to 4-pound) spaghetti squash, halved crosswise and seeded
¾ cup unsweetened plant-based milk
1 cup no-salt-added canned white beans, drained and rinsed
2 garlic cloves, smashed
2 tablespoons nutritional yeast (optional)

Grated zest and juice of 1 lemon
¼ teaspoon freshly ground black pepper
½ teaspoon kosher salt
5 ounces fresh baby spinach
1 (6-ounce) jar pitted kalamata olives, drained and chopped
2 or 3 jarred roasted red peppers, chopped
¼ cup chopped fresh flat-leaf parsley

1. Pour 1 cup water into the inner pot and insert a trivet. Place the squash on the trivet.

2. Lock the lid in place. Select Pressure Cook or Manual; adjust the pressure to High and the time to 8 minutes.

3. When cooking is complete, quick-release the pressure. Remove the lid and lift out the squash and trivet. Pour the water out of the inner pot and return it to the base.

4. Using a fork, scrape out the pulp of the squash, shredding it into long spaghetti-like strands. Discard the skin.

Continued >>

5. Add the milk, beans, garlic, nutritional yeast (if using), lemon zest, lemon juice, pepper, and salt to the inner pot. Use an immersion blender to puree the mixture. Stir in the squash strands.

6. Add the spinach, olives, and roasted peppers and toss to combine. Stir in half the parsley.

7. Serve hot, garnished with the remaining parsley.

SUBSTITUTION TIP: Frozen chopped spinach can be used instead of fresh. Thaw and drain it thoroughly; you'll want about 1 cup.

Per Serving: Calories: 279; Fat: 14g; Protein: 6g; Total carbohydrates: 35g; Fiber: 8g; Sugar: 9.5g; Sodium: 1,002mg

Tex-Mex Sweet Potato and Black Bean Stew

30-MINUTE • DAIRY-FREE • ONE-POT MEAL • VEGETARIAN

Serves 4

Prep time:
10 minutes

Pressure cook:
6 minutes

Release:
Quick

Total time:
30 minutes

Whether you call it vegetarian chili or Tex-Mex stew, this is a quick, delicious meal that's sure to please. For a milder dish, use the bell pepper instead of the poblano and omit the chipotle powder; if you like your food spicier, use poblano chiles and season away!

2 (15-ounce) cans black beans, drained and rinsed

1 large sweet potato (about 1 pound), peeled and cut into ½-inch pieces

1 cup chopped onion

½ cup chopped poblano or green bell pepper

2 teaspoons minced garlic

1 teaspoon kosher salt

2 tablespoons chili powder

½ teaspoon ground cumin

½ teaspoon chipotle powder (optional)

⅓ cup Vegetable Broth (page 148) or store-bought low-sodium vegetable broth

1 (14.5-ounce) can diced tomatoes

1 avocado, sliced (optional)

1 bunch cilantro, chopped (optional)

1 lime, cut into wedges (optional)

1. In the inner pot, combine the beans, sweet potato, onion, poblano, garlic, salt, chili powder, cumin, chipotle powder (if using), broth, and tomatoes.

2. Lock the lid into place. Select Pressure Cook or Manual; adjust the pressure to High and the time to 6 minutes.

3. When cooking is complete, quick-release the pressure. Remove the lid. Stir the stew and adjust the seasoning.

4. Ladle into bowls and serve with any garnishes desired, such as avocado, chopped cilantro, and lime wedges.

Per Serving: Calories: 280; Fat: 0.5g; Protein: 13g; Total carbohydrates: 56g; Fiber: 16g; Sugar: 8g; Sodium: 1,178mg

Artichoke-Mushroom Orzo

5-INGREDIENT • 30-MINUTE • ONE-POT MEAL • QUICK PREP • VEGETARIAN

Serves 6

Prep time:
5 minutes

Pressure cook:
4 minutes

Release:
Quick

Total time:
25 minutes

Artichokes and mushrooms make a wonderful flavor combination, and this easy pasta dish proves that. Marinated artichokes give the dish a head start on flavoring and help keep the orzo from sticking together.

1½ cups water
12 ounces orzo pasta
1 (12-ounce) jar marinated quartered artichoke hearts, undrained
8 ounces sliced mushrooms

½ cup chopped onion
1 teaspoon kosher salt
¼ teaspoon freshly ground black pepper
1 cup grated Parmesan cheese

1. Pour 1½ cups water into the inner pot. Stir in the orzo, artichokes with the marinade, mushrooms, onion, and salt.

2. Lock the lid into place. Select Pressure Cook or Manual; adjust the pressure to High and the time to 4 minutes.

3. When cooking is complete, quick-release the pressure. Remove the lid and stir in the pepper and Parmesan.

4. Adjust the seasoning and serve.

   INGREDIENT TIP: Buy vegetarian Parmesan if you're strictly vegetarian.

   FLAVOR BOOST: For a creamier dish, stir in ¼ to ½ cup heavy cream with the cheese. Depending on the flavor of the artichoke marinade, you may want to add a squeeze of lemon juice as well.

Per Serving: Calories: 317; Fat: 8.5g; Protein: 12g; Total carbohydrates: 50g; Fiber: 2.5g; Sugar: 3.5g; Sodium: 577mg

Pimento Cheese Quiche

5-INGREDIENT · VEGETARIAN

Serves 4

Prep time:
7 minutes

Pressure cook:
17 minutes

Release:
Quick

Cooling time:
10 minutes

Total time:
40 minutes

Sharp cheddar cheese, red peppers, and a hint of onion give this creamy quiche the flavor of pimento cheese, a Southern staple. Though pimento (or pimiento) peppers are obviously traditional, I prefer Spanish piquillos for their deeper, more intense flavor. But any roasted red pepper will work fine in this recipe.

5 large eggs
1⅓ cups half-and-half
½ teaspoon kosher salt
⅛ teaspoon freshly ground white or black pepper
1 teaspoon granulated onion
Butter or cooking spray, for the baking dish

2 cups grated sharp cheddar cheese
½ cup chopped piquillo peppers, pimiento peppers, or roasted red peppers
1 cup water

1. In a medium bowl, whisk the eggs until the yolks and whites are completely mixed. Add the half-and-half, salt, white pepper, and granulated onion and whisk to combine.

2. Coat the bottom and sides of a 1½-quart baking dish with butter or mist with cooking spray. Sprinkle half the cheddar over the bottom of the dish. Top with the chopped peppers, then add the remaining cheese. Carefully pour the custard over the cheese. Cover the dish with a square of foil. Do not crimp it down, because the quiche will expand; you just want to keep moisture off the top.

3. Add 1 cup of water to the inner pot and insert a trivet with handles. Place the baking dish on the trivet.

4. Lock the lid into place. Select Pressure Cook or Manual; adjust the pressure to High and the time to 17 minutes.

5. When cooking is complete, quick-release the pressure.

6. Remove the lid and lift out the quiche and trivet. The center may not be quite set, but it will firm up as it cools. Let the quiche cool and set for about 10 minutes before slicing and serving.

VARIATION: Quiche is the perfect vehicle for variations. Try roasted green chiles and Monterey Jack cheese for a Southwestern taste, or Gruyère and sautéed onions for a traditional French quiche.

Per Serving: Calories: 448; Fat: 36g; Protein: 24g; Total carbohydrates: 7g; Fiber: 0.5g; Sugar: 4.5g; Sodium: 651mg

Pasta Primavera

ONE-POT MEAL • VEGETARIAN

Serves 4

Prep time:
6 minutes

Sauté:
5 minutes

Pressure cook:
5 minutes

Release:
Quick

Total time:
40 minutes

New York's famed Le Cirque restaurant is supposed to have "invented" pasta primavera, though it's hard to believe that theirs was the first pairing of spring vegetables, pasta, and a light, creamy sauce. My version, which includes asparagus, broccoli, and cherry tomatoes, is so quick and easy that you'll never again need to go out to a restaurant for this delightful dinner.

1 bunch asparagus, trimmed
 and cut into 1-inch pieces
2 cups small broccoli florets
3½ cups water, divided
1½ teaspoons kosher salt,
 divided

12 ounces penne, farfalle,
 or rotini
½ cup heavy cream
1 cup cherry tomatoes, halved
½ cup grated Parmesan
 cheese, plus more for serving
¼ cup chopped fresh basil

1. Place the asparagus and broccoli florets in a steamer basket. Add 1 cup of water to the inner pot and place the steamer basket inside.

2. Lock the lid into place. Select Steam; adjust the pressure to High and time to 0 minutes. (Cooking for "0" minutes might seem strange, but by the time the pot comes to pressure, they're done!)

3. When cooking is complete, quick-release the pressure. Remove the lid and remove the steamer basket. Sprinkle the vegetables with ¼ teaspoon of the salt. Set aside.

4. Pour the water out of the inner pot and return the pot to the base. Add the pasta, 2½ cups of water, and the remaining 1¼ teaspoons of salt.

5. Lock the lid into place. Select Pressure Cook or Manual; adjust the pressure to High and the time to 5 minutes.

6. When cooking is complete, quick-release the pressure. Remove the lid.

7. Select Sauté and adjust the heat to Low. Add the cream, tomatoes, asparagus, broccoli, and Parmesan. Stir to combine. Bring to a simmer and cook until the tomatoes are warmed through and the sauce is thickened.

8. Ladle into bowls and garnish with the basil and additional cheese.

INGREDIENT TIP: Buy vegetarian Parmesan if you're strictly vegetarian.

EVEN EASIER: If you like, use thawed frozen asparagus and broccoli florets instead of fresh. Skip the vegetable steaming steps, cook the pasta as directed, then add the vegetables along with the cream, tomatoes, and Parmesan.

Per Serving: Calories: 520; Fat: 17g; Protein: 20g; Total carbohydrates: 74g; Fiber: 6.5g; Sugar: 7.5g; Sodium: 713mg

Mixed Vegetable "Fried" Rice

DAIRY-FREE • ONE-POT MEAL • VEGETARIAN

Serves 4

Though this vegan recipe isn't a true fried rice, it does provide the flavor profile of the original concept, but with much less work. A variety of frozen stir-fry vegetables can be found in most grocery stores, so you can choose your favorite combination.

Prep time:
6 minutes

Sauté:
5 minutes

Pressure cook:
4 minutes

Release:
Natural
(10 minutes),
then quick

Total time:
40 minutes

1 tablespoon vegetable oil
½ cup chopped scallions
  (2 to 4)
2 teaspoons minced garlic
1 teaspoon minced fresh ginger
1¼ cups jasmine or long-grain
  white rice, rinsed
1¼ cups water

½ teaspoon kosher salt
2 tablespoons soy sauce
2 teaspoons toasted sesame oil
1 teaspoon chili-garlic sauce or
  sriracha (optional)
2 cups frozen stir-fry
  vegetables, thawed

1. Select Sauté and adjust the heat to Medium. Add the oil to the inner pot and heat until shimmering or the display reads "Hot." Add the scallions and cook, stirring, for 1 minute or until they begin to soften. Add the garlic and ginger and cook for 30 seconds, until fragrant. Press Cancel.

2. Stir in the rice, water, and salt.

3. Lock the lid. Select Pressure Cook or Manual; adjust the pressure to High and the time to 4 minutes.

4. When cooking is complete, let the pressure release naturally for 10 minutes, then quick-release any remaining pressure.

5. Remove the lid and stir in the soy sauce, sesame oil, chili-garlic sauce (if using), and the vegetables. Set the lid back on top (no need to lock it) and select Keep Warm. Let the vegetables warm for 3 to 4 minutes before serving.

Per Serving: Calories: 277; Fat: 5.5g; Protein: 6g; Total carbohydrates: 51g; Fiber: 1.5g; Sugar: 2g; Sodium: 623mg

Polenta with Mushroom Sauce

VEGETARIAN

Serves 4

Prep time:
10 minutes

Sauté:
5 minutes

Pressure cook:
15 minutes

Release:
Natural
(10 minutes),
then quick

Total time:
50 minutes

Marinara sauce and onions give a boost of flavor to this hearty mushroom sauce. Served over cheese-enriched polenta, it makes a delicious and elegant entrée. Best of all—everything cooks in the same pot at the same time!

⅓ cup dry red or white wine
1 cup sliced onion
2 pounds mushrooms (any mixture), sliced
2 cups Marinara Sauce (page 152) or store-bought marinara sauce
1 teaspoon kosher salt, divided
1 cup polenta or grits (not instant or quick-cooking)

2 cups whole milk
1½ cups Vegetable Broth (page 148) or store-bought low-sodium vegetable broth
2 tablespoons unsalted butter
½ cup grated Parmesan cheese, plus more for finishing

1. Select Sauté and adjust the heat to Medium. Pour in the wine and let simmer for about 3 minutes or until reduced by about half.

2. Add the onion, mushrooms, marinara sauce, and ¼ teaspoon of salt and stir to combine. Place a tall trivet in the pot (tall enough to clear the mushroom mixture).

3. Pour the polenta into a heatproof bowl that holds at least 4 cups. Add the milk, broth, and remaining ¾ teaspoon of salt and stir. Place the bowl on top of the trivet.

4. Lock the lid into place. Select Pressure Cook or Manual; adjust the pressure to High and the time to 15 minutes.

5. When cooking is complete, let the pressure release naturally for 10 minutes, then quick-release any remaining pressure. Remove the lid.

Continued >>

6. Carefully remove the bowl of polenta. Stir the polenta (it may be clumpy at first). Add the butter and Parmesan to the polenta and stir again to melt the butter and cheese. Taste and adjust seasoning. Set aside.

7. Stir the mushroom sauce and taste for seasoning. If it's too thin, select Sauté and adjust the heat to Medium. Simmer until the sauce has thickened.

8. To serve, spoon the polenta into bowls and top with the mushroom sauce. Sprinkle with additional cheese, if desired.

INGREDIENT TIP: Buy vegetarian Parmesan if you're strictly vegetarian.

FLAVOR BOOST: Add ¼ teaspoon red pepper flakes and ½ teaspoon fennel seeds with the marinara to mimic the flavor of Italian sausage.

Per Serving: Calories: 500; Fat: 20g; Protein: 18g; Total carbohydrates: 62g; Fiber: 5.5g; Sugar: 16g; Sodium: 942mg

Spicy Chickpeas with Sun-Dried Tomatoes and Olives

30-MINUTE • DAIRY-FREE • ONE-POT MEAL • QUICK PREP • VEGETARIAN

Serves 4

Prep time:
5 minutes

Sauté:
4 minutes

Pressure cook:
6 minutes

Release:
Quick

Total time:
30 minutes

Inspired by the popular chickpea stews of North Africa, this dish gets a kick from harissa, a sauce made from red chiles, spices, and garlic. Different brands vary in spice level, so start with a little and add more to taste.

2 (15-ounce) cans chickpeas, drained and rinsed
1 cup chopped onion
1 tablespoon minced garlic
1 (14.5-ounce) can diced tomatoes
¼ cup chopped oil-packed sun-dried tomatoes

½ cup Vegetable Broth (page 148) or store-bought low-sodium vegetable broth
1 tablespoon harissa, or more to taste
6 ounces baby spinach
½ cup pitted kalamata olives

1. In the inner pot, combine the chickpeas, onion, garlic, diced tomatoes, sun-dried tomatoes, and broth.

2. Lock the lid into place. Select Pressure Cook or Manual; adjust the pressure to High and the time to 6 minutes.

3. When cooking is complete, quick-release the pressure. Remove the lid.

4. Select Sauté and adjust the heat to Low. Add the harissa, spinach, and olives and simmer for 2 to 3 minutes, until the spinach is wilted.

5. Adjust the seasoning and serve.

SUBSTITUTION TIP: Though chickpeas are traditional, you can also use white beans if you prefer.

Per Serving: Calories: 285; Fat: 9.5g; Protein: 11g; Total carbohydrates: 40g; Fiber: 10g; Sugar: 9g; Sodium: 800mg

Tofu and Vegetables with Coconut-Cilantro Sauce

30-MINUTE • DAIRY-FREE • ONE-POT MEAL • VEGETARIAN

Serves 4

The sauce for this unusual but tasty dish gets its lovely bright green color from cilantro and jalapeño, which complement the mild tofu.

Prep time:
10 minutes

Pressure cook:
3 minutes

Release:
Quick

Total time:
30 minutes

1 (14-ounce) can full-fat coconut milk
½ cup Vegetable Broth (page 148) or store-bought low-sodium vegetable broth
2 cups chopped fresh cilantro
1 tablespoon chopped jalapeño

1 scallion, chopped
½ teaspoon kosher salt
1 pound extra-firm tofu, cut into ½-inch cubes
6 ounces baby carrots
12 ounces broccoli florets

1. Pour the coconut milk into the inner pot. Add the broth, cilantro, jalapeño, scallion, and salt. Using an immersion blender, puree until mostly smooth. Add the tofu and carrots.

2. Lock the lid into place. Select Pressure Cook or Manual; adjust the pressure to High and the time to 3 minutes.

3. When cooking is complete, quick-release the pressure. Remove the lid and add the broccoli to the pot.

4. Lock the lid into place again. Select Pressure Cook or Manual; adjust the pressure to High and the time to 0 minutes. (Cooking for "0" minutes might seem strange, but by the time the pot comes to pressure, it's done!)

5. When cooking is complete, quick-release the pressure. Remove the lid and toss the tofu and vegetables to coat with sauce.

6. Adjust the seasoning. Scoop into bowls and serve.

Per Serving: Calories: 351; Fat: 28g; Protein: 16g; Total carbohydrates: 14g; Fiber: 6g; Sugar: 4g; Sodium: 225mg

Seafood and Poultry

Turkey Tenderloin with
Sun-Dried Tomato Pesto

5-INGREDIENT • 30-MINUTE

Serves 4

Prep time:
10 minutes

Pressure cook:
12 minutes

Release:
Quick

Total time:
30 minutes

Turkey tenderloins, a fairly modern cut of poultry, are boneless, skinless turkey breast meat sometimes cut into long portions similar to a pork tenderloin, and sometimes broader and wedge-shaped. They are usually sold in packs of two, and often packed in a salt solution (that is to say, brined), which both flavors them and keeps them moist as they cook. They cook quickly in the Instant Pot, and with the addition of a little pesto, make a delicious weeknight entrée.

2 turkey tenderloins
  (1½ pounds total)
Kosher salt (optional)
½ cup sun-dried tomato pesto,
  divided

1 cup Chicken Stock (page 147)
  or store-bought low-sodium
  chicken stock
2 tablespoons unsalted butter

1. If your turkey is not packaged in a salt solution, salt generously with kosher salt on all sides. Carefully cut the tenderloins lengthwise almost all the way through, stopping about ½ inch from the other side. Spread the turkey out like a book, then spread 2 tablespoons of the pesto over the cut sides of each tenderloin. Fold the tenderloins back together and spread 1½ tablespoons of pesto over the top of each.

2. Pour the stock into the inner pot and place a trivet inside. Place the tenderloins on the trivet.

3. Lock the lid into place. Select Pressure Cook or Manual; adjust the pressure to High and the time to 12 minutes.

4. When cooking is complete, quick-release the pressure. Remove the lid. Transfer the tenderloins to a cutting board and remove the trivet.

5. Add the remaining 1 tablespoon of pesto and butter to the stock in the pot, and stir until the butter is melted and emulsified.

6. To serve, cut the turkey into ¾-inch slices and drizzle the sauce over top.

SUBSTITUTION TIP: If you can't find sun-dried tomato pesto in your grocery store, combine 6 tablespoons regular pesto with 2 tablespoons puréed sun-dried tomatoes, or just use regular pesto.

Per Serving: Calories: 364; Fat: 21g; Protein: 41g; Total carbohydrates: 3g; Fiber: 0.5g; Sugar: 1.5g; Sodium: 706mg

Greek-Inspired Chicken and Quinoa

ONE-POT MEAL

Serves 4

Prep time:
10 minutes

Sauté:
4 minutes

Pressure cook:
3 minutes

Release:
Natural (10 minutes), then quick

Total time:
35 minutes

The pleasantly nutty flavor of quinoa nicely complements the Mediterranean flavors of tomatoes, kalamata olives, and feta cheese. The chicken breast cooks at the same time as the grain, so this delicious dinner comes together in just one pot.

2 tablespoons olive oil

1 cup chopped red onion

½ cup chopped red bell pepper

1 cup Chicken Stock (page 147) or store-bought low-sodium chicken stock

1½ pounds boneless, skinless chicken breast, cubed

¾ cup quinoa, well rinsed

1 teaspoon dried oregano

½ teaspoon kosher salt

½ teaspoon freshly ground black pepper

1 cup grape or cherry tomatoes, halved

½ cup pitted kalamata olives

¼ cup crumbled full-fat feta cheese

2 tablespoons fresh lemon juice

1. Select Sauté and adjust the heat to Medium. Pour in the olive oil. When the oil is hot, add the onion and bell pepper and cook, stirring occasionally, for 3 to 4 minutes, until softened. Press Cancel.

2. Add the stock, chicken, quinoa, oregano, salt, and black pepper.

3. Lock the lid in place. Select Pressure Cook or Manual; adjust the pressure to High and the time to 3 minutes.

4. When cooking is complete, let the pressure release naturally for 10 minutes, then quick-release any remaining pressure.

5. Remove the lid and stir in the tomatoes, olives, feta, and lemon juice

6. Serve hot.

Per Serving: Calories: 492; Fat: 20g; Protein: 46g; Total carbohydrates: 31g; Fiber: 4g; Sugar: 4.5g; Sodium: 663mg

Salmon and Vegetables with Lemon-Butter Sauce

ONE-POT MEAL

Serves 4

Prep time:
10 minutes

Pressure cook:
5 minutes

Release:
Natural
(8 minutes),
then quick

Total time:
35 minutes

Using frozen salmon fillets in the Instant Pot allows you to cook potatoes and carrots at the same time, so you can create a complete meal, tasty sauce and all, without a kitchenful of dishes to do after dinner.

½ cup Chicken Stock (page 147) or store-bought low-sodium chicken stock

1½ pounds medium red potatoes, quartered

4 carrots, peeled and cut into 1-inch-thick pieces (about 2 cups)

4 frozen salmon fillets (5 ounces each), do not thaw

4 tablespoons (½ stick) unsalted butter, melted

1½ teaspoons kosher salt

½ teaspoon garlic powder

Juice of 2 lemons

Freshly ground black pepper, for garnish

Chopped fresh dill, for garnish (optional)

1. Pour the broth into the inner pot and add the potatoes and carrots. Place the salmon fillets presentation-side up on top of the vegetables. Pour the melted butter over the salmon and sprinkle with the salt and garlic powder.

2. Lock the lid into place. Select Pressure Cook or Manual; set the pressure to High and the time to 5 minutes.

3. When cooking is complete, let the pressure release naturally for 8 minutes, then quick-release any remaining pressure.

4. Remove the lid and drizzle the lemon juice over everything.

5. Serve immediately garnished with black pepper and dill (if using).

Per Serving: Calories: 451; Fat: 21g; Protein: 32g; Total carbohydrates: 33g; Fiber: 4.5g; Sugar: 5g; Sodium: 566mg

Shredded Italian Chicken Sandwiches

30-MINUTE

Serves 4

Prep time:
8 minutes

Pressure cook:
9 minutes

Release:
Quick

Total time:
30 minutes

Marinara sauce and pesto give these chicken sandwiches tons of flavor with hardly any work. Chicken thighs cook quickly and stay juicy under pressure, making this a perfect family weeknight dinner.

Cooking spray
1½ pounds boneless, skinless chicken thighs (about 4 thighs)
½ teaspoon kosher salt
¾ cup Marinara Sauce (page 152) or store-bought marinara sauce

½ cup chopped roasted red peppers or piquillo peppers
2 tablespoons pesto
½ cup shredded mozzarella cheese, plus more (optional) for serving
4 sandwich or hamburger buns, sliced

1. Mist the bottom of the inner pot with cooking spray. Sprinkle the chicken on both sides with the salt and place in the inner pot. Add the marinara sauce.

2. Lock the lid into place. Select Pressure Cook or Manual; adjust the pressure to High and the time to 9 minutes.

3. When cooking is complete, quick-release the pressure. Remove the lid and use tongs to remove the chicken to a cutting board. If the sauce is very thin, select Sauté and adjust the heat to Low. Simmer until thickened.

4. Meanwhile, shred the meat, discarding any fat or gristle.

5. Return the chicken to the pot and add the roasted peppers, pesto, and mozzarella, stirring to melt the cheese.

6. Divide the chicken between the sandwich buns and serve. If you like, sprinkle a little more mozzarella cheese over the chicken.

Per Serving: Calories: 458; Fat: 19g; Protein: 43g; Total carbohydrates: 28g; Fiber: 2g; Sugar: 6g; Sodium: 835mg

Creole-Inspired Shrimp and Beans

30-MINUTE · DAIRY-FREE · ONE-POT MEAL · QUICK PREP

Serves 4

Prep time:
5 minutes

Sauté:
6 minutes

Pressure cook:
3 minutes

Release:
Quick

Total time:
30 minutes

One of the staples of New Orleans cuisine is the "holy trinity," a combination of chopped onions, celery, and bell pepper. Buying it already chopped saves time, but if you can't find it, make your own with 3 parts onion to 2 parts celery and pepper.

1 tablespoon vegetable oil or olive oil

4 ounces andouille sausage, chopped

2 teaspoons minced garlic

1½ cups "trinity" blend

1 (14.5-ounce) can diced tomatoes

2 (15-ounce) cans white beans, drained

2 teaspoons Cajun or Creole seasoning

½ teaspoon kosher salt (omit if seasoning mix contains salt)

1 pound peeled and deveined shrimp, thawed if frozen

1. Select Sauté and adjust the heat to High. Add the oil to the inner pot and heat until shimmering. Add the andouille and cook, stirring, until it begins to brown, about 2 minutes. Add the garlic and trinity and cook for 30 seconds or until fragrant. Press Cancel.

2. Add the tomatoes, beans, seasoning, and salt and stir to combine.

3. Lock the lid into place. Select Pressure Cook or Manual; adjust the pressure to High and the time to 3 minutes.

4. When cooking is complete, quick-release the pressure. Remove the lid.

5. Select Sauté and adjust the heat to Low. Add the shrimp and cook, stirring occasionally for about 3 minutes, until the shrimp are pink and opaque.

6. Adjust the seasoning. Ladle into bowls and serve.

Per Serving: Calories: 359; Fat: 8g; Protein: 38g; Total carbohydrates: 34g; Fiber: 14g; Sugar: 6g; Sodium: 1,095mg

Tandoori-Spiced Chicken and Rice

5-INGREDIENT • QUICK PREP

Serves 4

Prep time:
20 minutes

Pressure cook:
4 minutes

Release:
Natural
(10 minutes),
then quick

Total time:
45 minutes

A tandoor is an Indian clay oven that cooks at super-high temperatures, resulting in chicken that is lightly charred on the outside but tender and juicy inside. Though you can't get the crispy exterior in an Instant Pot, you can get the tandoori spice flavor.

4 boneless, skinless chicken thighs (about 1¼ pounds)
1½ teaspoons kosher salt, divided
¼ cup plain whole-milk Greek yogurt or homemade Yogurt (page 149)
1 tablespoon curry powder

2 teaspoons smoked or sweet paprika
¼ teaspoon freshly ground black pepper
1 cup basmati or long-grain white rice, rinsed
1 cup water

1. Sprinkle the chicken thighs on both sides with ¾ teaspoon of salt. Place in a zip-top plastic bag and set aside.

2. In a bowl, mix the yogurt, curry powder, paprika, and pepper until thoroughly combined. Pour the marinade over the chicken and manipulate the chicken to coat it with the sauce. Set aside for at least 15 minutes and up to 30 minutes to marinate.

3. Pour the rice into the inner pot. Add the water and remaining ¾ teaspoon of salt and stir to dissolve the salt. Remove the chicken thighs from the marinade and place on top of the rice. Drizzle the marinade over the chicken.

4. Lock the lid into place. Select Pressure Cook or Manual; adjust the heat to High and the time to 4 minutes.

5. When cooking is complete, let the pressure release naturally for 10 minutes, then quick-release any remaining pressure.

Per Serving: Calories: 360; Fat: 6g; Protein: 34g; Total carbohydrates: 40g; Fiber: 0g; Sugar: 0.5g; Sodium: 549mg

Scallion-Ginger Steamed Cod and Green Beans

30-MINUTE · **DAIRY-FREE** · **ONE-POT MEAL**

Serves 4

Prep time:
10 minutes

Steam:
3 minutes

Release:
Quick

Total time:
25 minutes

Whitefish, such as cod, steams quickly in the Instant Pot, and so do green beans, so this dish is a perfect match. The steaming liquid turns into a light, fragrant sauce for a one-pot meal that's sure to please.

4 cod fillets (6 ounces each), about 1 inch thick
1 teaspoon kosher salt
½ teaspoon ground white pepper
1 cup clam juice or seafood stock

½ bunch scallions (4 to 6 scallions), cut into 1-inch lengths
4 teaspoons minced fresh ginger
2 teaspoons fish sauce
8 ounces trimmed French green beans

1. Sprinkle the fish on both sides with the salt and white pepper.

2. Pour the clam juice into the inner pot. Add the scallions, ginger, and fish sauce and stir to combine. Place the green beans in a steamer basket and arrange the fish fillets on top. Place the steamer inside the pot.

3. Lock the lid into place. Select Pressure Cook or Manual; adjust the pressure to High and the time to 3 minutes.

4. When cooking is complete, quick-release the pressure. Remove the lid.

5. Transfer the fish and beans to a serving plate. Pour the broth over and serve.

   SUBSTITUTION TIP: Any firm whitefish will work in this recipe, such as halibut, grouper, snapper, or tilapia. To work with the cooking time here, you need to get 1-inch-thick fillets.

Per Serving: Calories: 165; Fat: 1g; Protein: 32g; Total carbohydrates: 5g; Fiber: 2g; Sugar: 2g; Sodium: 875mg

Basque-Inspired Chicken (Chicken Piperade)

30-MINUTE • DAIRY-FREE • ONE-POT MEAL • QUICK PREP

Serves 4

Prep time:
5 minutes

Sauté:
10 minutes

Pressure cook:
10 minutes

Release:
Quick

Total time:
45 minutes

If there's an iconic dish from the Basque region of northern Spain and southern France, it's got to be piperade. Bell peppers, tomatoes, and onions are flavored with the region's Espelette peppers, which are between paprika and cayenne in flavor (and so I have used both of those to mimic their taste). I also cook noodles along with the chicken and sauce, turning this into a hearty one-pot dinner.

4 bone-in, skin-on chicken thighs (about 2 pounds)

½ teaspoon kosher salt

1 tablespoon olive oil

1½ cups Chicken Stock (page 147) or store-bought low-sodium chicken stock, divided

1 (14.5-ounce) can diced tomatoes

1 tablespoon minced garlic

1½ teaspoons smoked or sweet paprika

¼ teaspoon cayenne pepper or hot paprika

2 tablespoons dry sherry or white wine

6 ounces egg noodles

1 (14-ounce) package frozen bell pepper and onion strips, thawed and drained

1. Sprinkle the chicken thighs with the salt. Set aside.

2. Select Sauté and adjust to the heat to High. Add the oil and heat until it shimmers or the display reads "Hot." Add the chicken thighs, skin-side down. Let them brown without moving for 5 minutes, then carefully lift one up to check the doneness. Cook until they are deep golden brown, rearranging as necessary so they brown evenly. When browned, turn and cook the other side for 2 to 3 minutes.

3. Remove the thighs to a cutting board and pour the fat out of the inner pot. Return the pot to the base and pour in ½ cup of chicken stock, scraping the bottom of the pot to get up any browned bits. Return the chicken to the pot, skin-side up.

4. Lock the lid into place. Select Pressure Cook or Manual; adjust the pressure to High and the time to 5 minutes.

5. When cooking is complete, quick-release the pressure. Remove the lid and transfer the thighs to the cutting board.

6. Pour the remaining 1 cup of chicken stock into the inner pot. Stir in the tomatoes, garlic, paprika, cayenne, and sherry. Add the noodles and press down so they are submerged.

7. Arrange the pepper/onion mixture and chicken, skin-side up, over the noodles.

8. Lock the lid into place. Select Pressure Cook or Manual; adjust the pressure to High and the time to 5 minutes.

9. When cooking is complete, quick-release the pressure. Remove the lid. The noodles should be just tender; if not, select Sauté and simmer for a minute or two until they're done.

10. Adjust the seasoning. Ladle into bowls and serve immediately.

EVEN EASIER: For a quicker weeknight dinner, use 1½ pounds boneless chicken thighs instead of bone-in. Skip the sautéing step and the initial pressure cooking of the chicken (steps 2 through 4). Instead, add the raw chicken to the pot over the noodles, and pressure cook for the 5 minutes as directed in step 8.

Per Serving: Calories: 552; Fat: 23g; Protein: 40g; Total carbohydrates: 43g; Fiber: 3.5g; Sugar: 8g; Sodium: 549mg

Smoked Salmon and Asparagus Risotto

30-MINUTE · ONE-POT MEAL · QUICK PREP

Serves 4

Prep time:
5 minutes

Sauté:
6 minutes

Pressure cook:
8 minutes

Release:
Quick

Total time:
30 minutes

Maybe you've never tried making risotto because you've heard it's time-consuming and fussy. Truth be told, it is when you make it the traditional way, but the Instant Pot turns it into an easy, almost hands-off meal. This version features smoked salmon and asparagus, making it an elegant, company-worthy entrée.

2 tablespoons unsalted butter, divided
½ cup chopped onion
1¼ cups arborio rice
⅓ cup white wine
3½ cups low-sodium chicken stock or vegetable broth, divided

½ teaspoon kosher salt
8 ounces frozen asparagus spears, thawed
6 ounces smoked salmon, flaked
¼ cup grated Parmesan cheese

1. Select Sauté and adjust the heat to Medium. Add 1 tablespoon of butter. When it has stopped foaming, add the onion and cook, stirring, for about 2 minutes, or until the onion pieces begin to separate and soften. Add the rice and stir to coat, cooking for about a minute. Add the wine and cook, stirring, for 2 to 3 minutes, until it's almost evaporated. Add 3 cups of stock and the salt and stir to combine.

2. Lock the lid into place. Select Pressure Cook or Manual; adjust the pressure to High and the time to 8 minutes.

3. While the rice cooks, drain any water from the asparagus and slice it on the diagonal into pieces about ½ inch long.

4. When cooking is complete, quick-release the pressure. Remove the lid and test the risotto; the rice should be soft with a slightly firm center, but not quite done. Select Sauté and adjust the heat to Low. If the rice is still very firm, simmer for a minute or two until more tender before adding the Parmesan, remaining ½ cup of stock, and remaining 1 tablespoon of butter. Stir until the butter is melted and the rice has loosened up.

5. Add the asparagus and salmon and cook to heat through, simmering if necessary to finish cooking the rice. Taste and adjust the seasoning.

VARIATION: Risotto is one of those dishes that adapts almost endlessly. Substitute cooked mushrooms and spinach or ham and peas for the salmon and asparagus.

Per Serving: Calories: 386; Fat: 13g; Protein: 16g; Total carbohydrates: 53g; Fiber: 4g; Sugar: 1.5g; Sodium: 592mg

Shrimp Boil

30-MINUTE • DAIRY-FREE • ONE-POT MEAL • QUICK PREP

Serves 4

Prep time:
5 minutes

Pressure cook:
7 minutes

Release:
Quick

Total time:
30 minutes

A traditional shrimp boil with potatoes, corn, and spicy sausage makes a fun family meal. Cooking it in the Instant Pot makes it easy, with very little prep and almost no cleanup. If you can't find fresh corn already shucked, frozen corn on the cob will work great in this recipe.

1 cup Chicken Stock (page 147) or store-bought low-sodium chicken stock

1 pound baby red potatoes, halved

4 links andouille sausage, sliced

4 ears corn, shucked and halved crosswise

1 tablespoon Cajun seasoning

1 pound frozen shell-on shrimp (do not thaw)

¼ cup chopped fresh parsley

1 lemon, cut into wedges

1. In the inner pot, combine the stock, potatoes, sausage, corn, and Cajun seasoning.

2. Lock the lid in place. Select Pressure Cook or Manual; adjust the pressure to High and the time to 5 minutes.

3. When cooking is complete, quick-release the pressure. Remove the lid and add the shrimp.

4. Lock the lid in place again. Select Pressure Cook or Manual; adjust the pressure to High and the time to 2 minutes.

5. When cooking is complete, quick-release the pressure. Remove the lid and stir in the parsley.

6. Serve with lemon wedges.

   SUBSTITUTION TIP: For a pescatarian version of this recipe, increase the shrimp to 2 pounds, omit the sausage, and replace the chicken stock with low-sodium vegetable broth.

Per Serving: Calories: 574; Fat: 26g; Protein: 38g; Total carbohydrates: 52g; Fiber: 5g; Sugar: 10g; Sodium: 1,423mg

Beef and Pork

Green Curry Pork

5-INGREDIENT • 30-MINUTE • DAIRY-FREE • ONE-POT MEAL

Serves 4

Prep time:
10 minutes

Pressure cook:
3 minutes

Release:
Quick

Total time:
30 minutes

Thai curry paste and canned coconut milk add loads of flavor to this simple curry. Because the pork tenderloin cooks so quickly, you'll have a delicious complete meal on the table in no time.

1 (13.5-ounce) can full-fat coconut milk
⅓ cup water
4 tablespoons Thai green curry paste
1 pound pork tenderloin, sliced about ½ inch thick

4 carrots, cut into thick coins
10 ounces green beans, trimmed
1 tablespoon maple syrup or coconut sugar (optional)

1. In the inner pot, combine the coconut milk, water, and curry paste. Mix the ingredients together until smooth. Add the pork, carrots, and green beans (there's no need to mix them with the sauce).

2. Lock the lid in place. Select Pressure Cook or Manual; adjust the pressure to High and the time to 3 minutes.

3. When cooking is complete, quick-release the pressure. Remove the lid. Sir in the maple syrup or coconut sugar (if using).

4. Adjust the seasoning and serve.

SUBSTITUTION TIP: For a vegan version of this curry, replace the pork with a large diced sweet potato and add 2 cups of frozen thawed broccoli florets after the curry cooks, stirring to warm through. The cook time remains the same.

Per Serving: Calories: 382; Fat: 23g; Protein: 28g; Total carbohydrates: 20g; Fiber: 4.5g; Sugar: 8g; Sodium: 620mg

Pork Tenderloin with Cabbage and Noodles

DAIRY-FREE · ONE-POT MEAL · QUICK PREP

Serves 4

Prep time:
5 minutes

Sauté:
7 minutes

Pressure cook:
4 minutes

Release:
Quick

Total time:
35 minutes

The classic Eastern European dish of cabbage and noodles pairs wonderfully with seared pork tenderloin, resulting in a complete meal that's easy enough for a weeknight but elegant enough for a Sunday dinner.

1 tablespoon vegetable oil or olive oil
1 pork tenderloin (about 1¼ pounds)
1½ teaspoons kosher salt, divided, plus more to taste
¼ teaspoon freshly ground black pepper, plus more to taste
1 teaspoon smoked or regular paprika
1 cup sliced onion
4 cups shredded green cabbage or coleslaw mix
⅓ cup dry white wine
1½ cups Chicken Stock (page 147) or store-bought low-sodium chicken stock
6 ounces wide egg noodles

1. Select Sauté and adjust the heat to High. Add the oil and heat until shimmering or the display reads "Hot." While it heats, cut the tenderloin in half crosswise (so it fits in the pot more easily). Sprinkle the pork with 1 teaspoon of salt, the pepper, and the paprika. When the oil is hot, add the pork tenderloin and sear, undisturbed, until browned, 2 to 3 minutes, then turn and sear the other sides. Transfer to a cutting board.

2. Add the onion and cabbage to the pot and stir to coat with the remaining fat. Add the wine and bring to a simmer, scraping up any browned bits from the bottom of the pot. Let the wine reduce slightly.

3. Add the chicken stock and noodles and stir to cover the noodles with the liquid (add more stock if the noodles are not submerged). Place the pork tenderloin on top of the vegetables and noodles.

4. Lock the lid into place. Select Pressure Cook or Manual; adjust the pressure to Low and the time to 4 minutes.

5. When cooking is complete, quick-release the pressure. Remove the lid and check the temperature of the pork; it should be about 145°F. If it is much lower than that, put it back with the noodles and put the lid on but don't lock it into place. Check it again in a couple of minutes.

6. When it's done, transfer the pork to a cutting board and let it rest for a couple of minutes. Taste the noodles and cabbage and adjust the seasoning, adding more salt and pepper if necessary, then spoon into a serving dish.

7. Slice the pork and serve with the cabbage and noodles.

VARIATION: This recipe also works well with turkey tenderloin in place of the pork. Cooking time remains the same.

Per Serving: Calories: 402; Fat: 8.5g; Protein: 39g; Total carbohydrates: 38g; Fiber: 4g; Sugar: 5g; Sodium: 594mg

Ramen with Pork and Snow Peas

DAIRY-FREE • ONE-POT MEAL • QUICK PREP

Serves 4

Prep time:
5 minutes

Pressure cook:
25 minutes

Release:
Quick

Total time:
45 minutes

If your experience with ramen is only the instant packs familiar to college students, you'll be surprised at how flavorful this dish is when made from scratch. Pressure cooking pork shoulder yields an intense, silky, rich broth as a base, while the noodles and snow peas cook almost instantly for a warming, tasty weeknight dinner.

1¼ pounds boneless pork country shoulder ribs or pork shoulder

6 scallions, divided

1 teaspoon minced fresh ginger

2 teaspoons gochujang or chili-garlic sauce

2 tablespoons soy sauce

4½ cups Chicken Stock (page 147) or store-bought low-sodium chicken stock, divided

8 ounces dried ramen or Chinese wheat noodles

8 ounces snow peas, trimmed

1 tablespoon toasted sesame seeds

1. If using pork shoulder, cut it into chunks or strips about 2 inches thick. Place the pork in the inner pot. Add 2 of the whole scallions, the ginger, the gochujang, the soy sauce, and 4 cups of stock. Stir to combine.

2. Lock the lid into place. Select Pressure Cook or Manual; adjust the pressure to High and the time to 25 minutes.

3. While the pork cooks, cut the remaining scallions into thin slices, keeping the white and green parts separate.

4. When cooking is complete, quick-release the pressure. Remove the lid and use tongs to remove the pork to a cutting board. Discard the whole scallions.

5. Stir in the remaining ½ cup of stock (this helps cool down the broth in the pot so the lid will go on). Add the noodles, scallion whites, and snow peas.

6. Lock the lid into place. Select Pressure Cook or Manual; adjust the pressure to High and the time to 0 minutes. (Cooking for "0" minutes might seem strange, but by the time the pot comes to pressure, they're done!)

7. While the noodles cook, shred the pork, discarding any fat or gristle.

8. When cooking is complete, quick-release the pressure. Remove the lid and stir to separate the noodles. Add the pork to the pot and taste the broth, adjusting the seasonings as necessary.

9. Ladle into bowls and garnish with the scallion greens and sesame seeds.

FLAVOR BOOST: Ramen is often served with slices of eggs cooked until firm with slightly soft yolks. If you like, pressure steam 4 eggs for 5 minutes with quick release, then cool and peel the eggs. At serving, slice the eggs and divide between the bowls.

Per Serving: Calories: 542; Fat: 21g; Protein: 40g; Total carbohydrates: 46g; Fiber: 3g; Sugar: 8.5g; Sodium: 1,241mg

Lazy Lasagna

5-INGREDIENT

Serves 4

Prep time:
10 minutes

Sauté:
5 minutes

Pressure cook:
8 minutes

Release:
Quick

Total time:
40 minutes

I love traditional lasagna, with homemade noodles, homemade sauce, and homemade béchamel. My partner, Dave, and I make it once a year or so, when we have a day to devote to all the components and a couple of hours to wait while it cooks. In between times, we rely on this quick facsimile, which is not traditional but is delicious and—best of all—really easy.

Cooking spray

1 pound sweet or hot Italian sausage, casings removed

1½ cups water

8 ounces lasagna noodles, broken into 4 to 6 pieces each

2½ cups Marinara Sauce (page 152) or store-bought marinara sauce

¼ teaspoon kosher salt

6 ounces whole-milk ricotta cheese, at room temperature

½ cup grated Parmesan cheese, plus more (optional) for serving

¼ teaspoon freshly ground black pepper

1. Mist the inner pot with cooking spray. Select Sauté and adjust the heat to High. Add the sausage to the pot and break it up into bite-size chunks with a spoon or spatula. Let it brown for 2 to 3 minutes, stirring occasionally (it won't be completely cooked). Press Cancel.

2. Pour the water into the pot and scrape up any browned meat from the bottom of the pot. Add the broken lasagna noodles, the marinara sauce, and salt. Stir to combine, and push the noodles down into the liquid.

3. Lock the lid into place. Select Pressure Cook or Manual; adjust the pressure to High and the time to 8 minutes.

4. Meanwhile, in a small bowl, mix together the ricotta, Parmesan, and pepper.

5. After cooking is complete, quick-release the pressure. Remove the lid. Test the pasta; it should be tender with just a slightly firm center. If not, select Sauté and simmer for a few minutes until it finishes cooking.

6. To serve, ladle into bowls and top each bowl with a spoonful of the ricotta mixture, swirling it through the pasta. Sprinkle with more Parmesan, if desired.

INGREDIENT TIP: Buy vegetarian Parmesan if you're strictly vegetarian.

SUBSTITUTION TIP: For a vegetarian version, substitute quartered mushrooms for the sausage. The cooking time remains the same.

Per Serving: Calories: 614; Fat: 31g; Protein: 27g; Total carbohydrates: 58g; Fiber: 6g; Sugar: 7g; Sodium: 991mg

Sloppy Joes

DAIRY-FREE • ONE-POT MEAL • QUICK PREP

Serves 8

Both kids and adults will love these savory sandwiches. For a low-carb option, skip the bun and serve the beef with slaw.

Prep time:
5 minutes

Sauté:
5 minutes

Pressure cook:
10 minutes

Release:
Natural
(10 minutes),
then quick

Total time:
40 minutes

1 tablespoon extra-virgin olive oil

2 pounds ground beef (90% lean)

1 teaspoon chili powder

1 teaspoon onion powder

½ teaspoon garlic powder

1 (15-ounce) can tomato puree

½ cup ketchup

2 tablespoons reduced-sodium soy sauce

1 tablespoon brown sugar

8 hamburger buns, split

Shredded red cabbage, for garnish (optional)

Chopped fresh parsley, for garnish (optional)

1. Select Sauté and adjust the heat to High. Add the olive oil and heat until shimmering. Add the ground beef and cook for 3 minutes, using a spatula to break up the meat.

2. Press Cancel and add the chili powder, onion powder, garlic powder, tomato puree, ketchup, soy sauce, and brown sugar. Stir to combine.

3. Lock the lid into place. Select Pressure Cook or Manual; set the pressure to High and the time to 10 minutes.

4. When cooking is complete, let the pressure release naturally for 10 minutes, then quick-release any remaining pressure.

5. Remove the lid. Stir the Sloppy Joe mixture to make sure it's well combined, and adjust the seasoning.

6. Serve immediately on buns. If desired, garnish with red cabbage and parsley.

Per Serving: Calories: 386; Fat: 15g; Protein: 28g; Total carbohydrates: 34g; Fiber: 2g; Sugar: 12g; Sodium: 704mg

Italian Beef

5-INGREDIENT • ONE-POT MEAL • QUICK PREP

Serves 6

Prep time:
5 minutes

Pressure cook:
45 minutes

Release:
Quick

Total time:
1 hour
10 minutes

If you've ever visited Chicago, you've probably seen Italian beef sandwiches for sale in many neighborhoods. Cooked with green bell peppers and pickled hot peppers, the beef is flavorful and juicy. But you don't have to visit Chicago to sample this delicious treat. You can make it at home with little effort and a handful of ingredients. Serve this on its own or over polenta or mashed potatoes.

1 chuck roast (3 pounds), about 3 inches thick
1 teaspoon kosher salt
1 (10.5-ounce) can condensed beef consommé
1 tablespoon Italian seasoning

1 cup sliced hot pickled banana peppers or pepperoncini with 2 tablespoons juice
1 (14-ounce) package frozen sliced onions and peppers, thawed

1. Sprinkle both sides of the chuck roast with the salt, then transfer it to the inner pot. Add the consommé, Italian seasoning, pickled peppers and juice, and onion and pepper mix.

2. Lock the lid into place. Select Pressure Cook or Manual; adjust the pressure to High and the time to 45 minutes.

3. When cooking is complete, quick-release the pressure. Remove the lid. Transfer the meat to a cutting board and use two forks to shred the meat into chunks, discarding any fat or gristle.

4. Return the beef to the sauce, adjust the seasoning, and serve.

FLAVOR BOOST: For Italian beef sandwiches, spoon some beef and peppers into sliced hoagie rolls and top with sliced provolone cheese. Serve with the sauce on the side for dipping.

Per Serving: Calories: 596; Fat: 42g; Protein: 45g; Total carbohydrates: 5g; Fiber: 0.5g; Sugar: 2.5g; Sodium: 903mg

Beef Stroganoff

ONE-POT MEAL • QUICK PREP

Serves 4

Prep time:
5 minutes

Sauté:
8 minutes

Pressure cook:
27 minutes

Release:
Quick

Total time:
55 minutes

When I was growing up, beef stroganoff was one of my mom's standby "company" dinners. For me, it still retains an air of elegance, although my streamlined recipe with mushrooms, noodles, and sauce all in one pot means you don't have to wait for company to make it.

1 tablespoon vegetable oil
1 pound beef mock tenders or petit tenders
½ teaspoon kosher salt
⅓ cup dry sherry or white wine
1 (10.5-ounce) can condensed beef consommé

6 ounces egg noodles
8 ounces button or cremini mushrooms, sliced
1 cup sliced onions
¼ teaspoon freshly ground black pepper
⅓ cup sour cream

1. Select Sauté and adjust the heat to High. Add the oil to the inner pot and heat until shimmering or the display reads "Hot." While the oil heats, sprinkle the beef on all sides with the salt. When the oil is hot, add the beef and sear without moving for 2 to 3 minutes, until dark brown. Turn and brown the other side. Transfer the beef to a rack or cutting board and set aside to cool slightly.

2. Add the sherry to the pot and stir, scraping the bottom of the pan to dissolve the browned bits. Bring to a boil and cook for 1 to 2 minutes, until the sherry has reduced by about one-third.

3. While the sherry reduces, cut the beef into slices about ½ inch thick.

4. When the sherry has reduced, return the beef to the pot. Add the consommé and scrape up any browned bits to incorporate.

5. Lock the lid into place. Select Pressure Cook or Manual; adjust the pressure to High and the time to 22 minutes.

6. When cooking is complete, quick-release the pressure. Remove the lid and stir the noodles into the liquid. Add the mushrooms and onions.

7. Lock the lid into place again. Select Pressure Cook or Manual; adjust the pressure to High and the time to 5 minutes.

8. When cooking is complete, quick-release the pressure. Remove the lid and stir in the pepper and sour cream. Taste and adjust the seasonings, then serve immediately.

SUBSTITUTION TIP: For a dairy-free dish, omit the sour cream and stir in 1 teaspoon cornstarch dissolved in 1 tablespoon water after the noodles have cooked. Bring to a simmer and stir until thickened.

Per Serving: Calories: 449; Fat: 17g; Protein: 35g; Total carbohydrates: 37g; Fiber: 2.5g; Sugar: 4.5g; Sodium: 650mg

Teriyaki Pork Chops with Brown Rice

5-INGREDIENT • DAIRY-FREE • ONE-POT MEAL • QUICK PREP

Serves 4

Prep time:
20 minutes

Sauté:
5 minutes

Pressure cook:
22 minutes

Release:
Natural
(10 minutes),
then quick

Total time:
1 hour
15 minutes

In Japan, where teriyaki originated, the term refers to both a method of grilling and to the sauce that's basted over the meat as it browns. In the United States, sweet and savory soy-based sauces derived from the Japanese original have become wildly popular, whether we're grilling or not, and many good-quality commercial versions are available. I like Kikkoman's Original Teriyaki Sauce.

1½ pounds bone-in pork shoulder chops or steaks
¾ cup teriyaki sauce, plus more (optional) for serving
¾ cup water
½ teaspoon kosher salt
1 cup brown rice, rinsed
1 cup frozen green peas, thawed

1. Place the pork in a zip-top bag and pour the teriyaki sauce over it to coat. Let it sit for at least 15 minutes or, if you have the time, up to overnight in the refrigerator.

2. Pour the water into the inner pot and stir in the salt. Add the rice and stir. Remove the pork from the sauce and place it over the rice. Drizzle with a few tablespoons of the teriyaki sauce. Discard the remaining marinade.

3. Lock the lid into place. Select Pressure Cook or Manual; adjust the pressure to High and the time to 22 minutes.

4. When cooking is complete, let the pressure release naturally for 10 minutes, then quick-release any remaining pressure.

5. Remove the lid. Transfer the pork to a cutting board or plate. Stir the peas into the rice to warm them through. If there is liquid in the rice, select Sauté and adjust the heat to Low. Simmer until the liquid is evaporated.

6. To serve, spoon the rice and peas onto a platter. Carve the pork off the bone and set on top. If desired, brush with additional teriyaki sauce.

FLAVOR BOOST: Because teriyaki is traditionally grilled or broiled, I like to brown the chops after pressure cooking. Transfer the pork to a broiler pan, then brush with the teriyaki sauce and broil for 2 to 3 minutes, until browned. Turn and brown the other side.

Per Serving: Calories: 402; Fat: 11g; Protein: 30g; Total carbohydrates: 43g; Fiber: 3g; Sugar: 4.5g; Sodium: 916mg

Spicy Beef Lettuce Wraps

30-MINUTE • DAIRY-FREE • ONE-POT MEAL

Serves 4 as a main dish, 8 as an appetizer

Ground beef and vegetables combine with a spicy sauce to make a tasty filling for lettuce leaves in this fast, easy dish. Alone, it's great for lunch or a light supper, or pair it with Mixed Vegetable "Fried" Rice (page 82) for a more substantial dinner.

Prep time:
7 minutes

Sauté:
7 minutes

Pressure cook:
4 minutes

Release:
Quick

Total time:
30 minutes

Cooking spray

1½ pounds ground beef (85% lean)

⅓ cup hoisin sauce

2 teaspoons chili-garlic sauce

2 teaspoons minced fresh ginger

1 (8-ounce) can water chestnuts, drained and chopped

½ cup chopped red bell pepper

3 scallions, chopped, white and green parts kept separate

1 to 2 heads butter or Boston lettuce

¼ cup chopped toasted almonds or peanuts, for garnish (optional)

2 tablespoons coarsely chopped fresh cilantro, for garnish (optional)

¼ cup chopped cucumber, for garnish (optional)

1. Mist the bottom of the inner pot with cooking spray. Select Sauté and adjust the heat to High. Add the beef to the pot and break it up with a spoon or spatula. Let it brown for 2 to 3 minutes, stirring occasionally. (It won't be cooked all the way.) Press Cancel.

2. Scrape up any browned bits from the bottom of the pot. Add the hoisin, chili-garlic sauce, ginger, water chestnuts, and bell pepper. Stir gently to combine.

3. Lock the lid into place. Select Pressure Cook or Manual; adjust the heat to High and the time to 4 minutes.

Continued >>

4. While the beef cooks, pull off the larger lettuce leaves to be used as wraps (discard any wilted or tough outer leaves, and set aside the very small inner leaves for another use). You'll want 4 to 5 leaves per person for an entrée, depending on the size of the leaves and your appetites. For an appetizer, figure on 2 smaller leaves per person.

5. When cooking is complete, quick-release the pressure. Remove the lid.

6. Select Sauté and adjust the heat to Medium. Stir in the scallion whites. Bring to a simmer and cook, stirring occasionally, for 2 to 3 minutes to thicken the sauce.

7. To serve, spoon some of the beef into each of the lettuce leaves. Top with the scallion greens and any optional toppings you like.

SUBSTITUTION TIP: These are also good with ground turkey or pork in place of the beef. Cooking time remains the same.

Per Serving (main dish): Calories: 550; Fat: 39g; Protein: 32g; Total carbohydrates: 19g; Fiber: 3g; Sugar: 9g; Sodium: 514mg

---

Per Serving (appetizer): Calories: 275; Fat: 19g; Protein: 16g; Total carbohydrates: 10g; Fiber: 1.5g; Sugar: 4.5g; Sodium: 257mg

Hoisin Beef and Broccoli

5-INGREDIENT • **DAIRY-FREE** • **ONE-POT MEAL** • **QUICK PREP**

Serves 4

Prep time:
5 minutes

Pressure cook:
26 minutes

Release:
Quick

Total time:
50 minutes

Beef "mock tenders" or "petit tenders" are cut from the shoulder. Unlike chuck roast, which contains several different muscles connected with fat and sinew, tenders are cut from a single muscle, which results in much less waste. An easy but complex sauce and quick-cooking broccoli turn this wonderful cut into a delicious Chinese American restaurant classic.

1 pound beef mock tenders or petit tenders
⅓ cup hoisin sauce
3 tablespoons water
1 tablespoon minced fresh ginger

1 teaspoon chili-garlic sauce
4 cups broccoli florets (about 14 ounces)
Steamed rice (optional), for serving

1. Slice the beef into bite-size pieces about ¼ inch thick.

2. In the inner pot, combine the hoisin sauce, water, ginger, and chili-garlic sauce. Add the beef, stirring to coat with the sauce.

3. Lock the lid into place. Select Pressure Cook or Manual; adjust the pressure to High and the time to 25 minutes.

4. When cooking is complete, quick-release the pressure. Remove the lid and stir the beef and sauce. Add the broccoli florets on top of the beef.

5. Lock the lid into place. Select Pressure Cook or Manual; adjust the pressure to High and the time to 1 minute.

6. When cooking is complete, quick-release the pressure. Remove the lid and gently stir the beef and broccoli to coat with sauce.

7. Serve alone or over steamed rice, if desired.

Per Serving: Calories: 252; Fat: 9g; Protein: 28g; Total carbohydrates: 16g; Fiber: 3g; Sugar: 8g; Sodium: 488mg

Desserts

Easy Frozen Berry Crisp

QUICK PREP • VEGETARIAN

Serves 6

Frozen mixed berries are one of my favorite ingredients. They make a great addition to yogurt or oatmeal for breakfast, an easy fruit sauce, or, as in this recipe, a deliciously easy dessert.

Prep time:
5 minutes

Pressure cook:
12 minutes

Release:
Natural

Cooling time:
5 minutes

Total time:
40 minutes

12 ounces frozen mixed berries (no need to thaw)
¼ cup granulated sugar
Grated zest of 1 lemon
3 tablespoons fresh lemon juice
¼ cup all-purpose flour

¼ cup rolled oats
¼ cup slivered almonds
1 tablespoon light brown sugar
½ teaspoon kosher salt
3 tablespoons unsalted butter, cut into thin slices
1 cup water

1. In a heatproof bowl or pan that fits in the inner pot, toss together the berries, granulated sugar, lemon zest, and lemon juice.

2. In a medium bowl, combine the flour, oats, almonds, brown sugar, and salt. Sprinkle the oatmeal topping over the frozen berries. Place the butter slices on top of the oatmeal topping and cover the bowl with foil.

3. Pour 1 cup of water into the pot and insert a trivet with handles. Place the covered bowl or pan on top.

4. Lock the lid into place. Select Pressure Cook or Manual; adjust the pressure to High and the time to 12 minutes.

5. When cooking is complete, let the pressure release naturally.

6. Remove the lid and lift out the bowl or pan and trivet. Remove the foil and let cool for a few minutes before serving.

Per Serving: Calories: 150; Fat: 8.5g; Protein: 3g; Total carbohydrates: 17g; Fiber: 3g; Sugar: 6.5g; Sodium: 96mg

Ramekin Brownies

30-MINUTE • QUICK PREP • VEGETARIAN

Serves 4

Who doesn't want their own personal brownie? These rich, chocolaty treats come together quickly for a special after-school snack, or top them with ice cream for a decadent dessert.

Prep time:
5 minutes

Pressure cook:
7 minutes

Release:
Natural
(7 minutes),
then quick

Cooling time:
5 minutes

Total time:
30 minutes

Cooking spray
½ cup all-purpose flour
6 tablespoons unsweetened cocoa powder
¼ cup sugar
½ teaspoon fine salt

4 tablespoons (½ stick) unsalted butter, melted
¼ cup whole milk
1 large egg
¼ cup chocolate chips
1 cup water

1. Mist the bottoms and sides of four 2-inch ramekins with cooking spray and set aside.

2. In a medium bowl, combine the flour, cocoa, sugar, and salt. Add the melted butter, milk, egg, and chocolate chips and mix well.

3. Divide the brownie batter between the ramekins (about ⅓ cup batter each). Cover each ramekin with foil.

4. Pour the water into the pot and insert a trivet with handles. Arrange the ramekins on the trivet, stacking as necessary.

5. Lock the lid into place. Select Pressure Cook or Manual; adjust the pressure to High and the time to 7 minutes.

6. When cooking is complete, let the pressure release naturally for 7 minutes, then quick-release any remaining pressure.

7. Remove the lid and lift the trivet and ramekins from the pot. Remove the foil and let the brownies cool for 5 minutes. Serve the brownies in the ramekins while still warm.

Per Serving: Calories: 325; Fat: 21g; Protein: 5.5g; Total carbohydrates: 36g; Fiber: 4g; Sugar: 19g; Sodium: 318mg

Strawberry Shortcake Pudding

5-INGREDIENT · VEGETARIAN

Serves 6

Prep time:
12 minutes

Pressure cook:
17 minutes

Release:
Quick

Cooling time:
10 minutes

Total time:
50 minutes

If you cross strawberry shortcake with bread pudding, this scrumptious dessert is the happy result. Store-bought pound cake and frozen berries make it easy and fast enough for a weeknight treat.

3 large eggs
1½ cups heavy cream, divided
¼ cup vanilla sugar, plus
   2 tablespoons
Pinch kosher salt

1 small pound cake (12 ounces),
   cut into 1-inch cubes (about
   4 cups)
3 cups frozen strawberries,
   thawed, divided
Cooking spray
1 cup water

1. In a large bowl, whisk together the eggs, ¾ cup of cream, ¼ cup of vanilla sugar, and the salt. Add the pound cake cubes and gently stir to coat with the custard mixture. Let sit for a few minutes, then toss again. Most of the custard should be absorbed. Fold in 1½ cups of strawberries.

2. Mist the bottom and sides of a 1½-quart baking dish with cooking spray. Spoon the cake/custard/strawberry mixture into the dish.

3. Pour 1 cup of water into the inner pot and insert a trivet with handles. Place the baking dish on the trivet and place a square of foil over the dish.

4. Lock the lid into place. Select Pressure Cook or Manual; adjust the pressure to High and the time to 17 minutes.

5. When cooking is complete, quick-release the pressure. Remove the lid and lift out the trivet and baking dish. Remove the foil and let cool for 10 minutes.

6. While the pudding cools, mash the remaining 1½ cups strawberries with 1 tablespoon of vanilla sugar.

7. In a medium bowl, with an electric mixer or whisk, whip the remaining ¾ cup of cream with the remaining 1 tablespoon of vanilla sugar until soft peaks form.

8. To serve, scoop out large spoonfuls of the pudding onto dessert plates. Top with the berries and whipped cream.

SUBSTITUTION TIP: Vanilla sugar can be found online, in gourmet stores, and in most large grocery stores. If you can't find it, use plain granulated sugar and add ½ teaspoon vanilla extract to the custard and ½ teaspoon to the cream before whipping.

Per Serving: Calories: 529; Fat: 35g; Protein: 8g; Total carbohydrates: 46g; Fiber: 1g; Sugar: 31g; Sodium: 222mg

Chai-Spiced Custards

5-INGREDIENT · VEGETARIAN

Serves 4

Prep time:
10 minutes

Pressure cook:
6 minutes

Release:
Natural
(10 minutes),
then quick

**Cooling/
Chilling
time:** 2 hours
20 minutes

Total time:
3 hours

If you're a fan of masala chai (often simply called chai), the South Asian spiced tea, this dessert will quickly become a favorite. The Instant Pot turns out silky custards with next to no effort—no need to stand at the stove stirring and tempering eggs. Just pour the spiced custard mixture into bowls, and the Instant Pot does the rest.

2 cups heavy cream	Pinch salt
1 large egg	1 teaspoon chai spice
4 large egg yolks	1 teaspoon vanilla extract
½ cup sugar	1 cup water

1. In a medium bowl, whisk together the cream, whole egg, and egg yolks until thoroughly combined. Whisk in the sugar, salt, chai spice, and vanilla.

2. Pour the custard mixture into four 1½-cup ramekins or custard cups.

3. Add 1 cup of water to the inner pot. Insert a trivet and place the ramekins on top, stacking if necessary. Drape a piece of foil over the ramekins.

4. Lock the lid into place. Select Pressure Cook or Manual; adjust the pressure to Low and the time to 6 minutes.

5. When cooking is complete, let the pressure release naturally for 10 minutes, then quick-release any remaining pressure. Remove the lid.

6. Carefully remove the foil and use tongs to remove the custards. Let cool at room temperature for 20 minutes or so, then refrigerate until chilled, about 2 hours.

Per Serving: Calories: 581; Fat: 49g; Protein: 8g; Total carbohydrates: 29g; Fiber: 0g; Sugar: 29g; Sodium: 93mg

Mulled Applesauce
Gingersnap Parfaits

5-INGREDIENT · VEGETARIAN

Serves 6

Prep time:
25 minutes

Pressure cook:
4 minutes

Release:
Natural
(15 minutes),
then quick

Chilling time:
20 minutes

Total time:
1 hour
20 minutes

When I was growing up, my mother had a few "company" desserts that seemed very fancy but required little effort. It seemed impossible that store-bought gingersnap cookies, applesauce, and whipped cream could turn into a beautiful and delicious parfait. In this version, I start by making homemade applesauce with the flavor of mulled cider, but it's still a snap to make.

1½ pounds McIntosh, Gala, or
    Jonathan apples
3 tablespoons water
2 tablespoons sugar, divided,
    plus more to taste

Pinch kosher salt
1 bag mulling spices
8 ounces gingersnaps (about
    32 cookies)
1 cup heavy (whipping) cream

1. Peel, halve, and core the apples. Cut each apple half into 4 wedges and cut each wedge in half to make chunks.

2. Place the apples in the inner pot. Add the water, 1 tablespoon of sugar, the salt, and the mulling spices. Stir to combine.

3. Lock the lid into place. Select Pressure Cook or Manual; adjust the pressure to High and the time to 4 minutes.

4. When cooking is complete, let the pressure release naturally for 15 minutes, then quick-release any remaining pressure. Remove the lid and discard the mulling spices.

5. Use a potato masher to break up the apples if you like chunky applesauce, or puree with an immersion blender if you prefer a smoother sauce. Taste and adjust the seasoning, adding more sugar if desired. Let cool to room temperature.

6. While the applesauce cools, crush the cookies into fine crumbs in a food processor or with a rolling pin.

Continued >>

7. Whip the cream until frothy with a hand mixer. Add the remaining 1 tablespoon of sugar and continue whipping until soft peaks form.

8. To assemble, spoon about 1 tablespoon of crumbs into the bottom of each of six small wineglasses. Add ¼-inch layers of the following (in this order): applesauce, whipped cream, gingersnap crumbs. Repeat this layering at least 3 times, until the glasses are full (or you run out of ingredients). Top with a sprinkling of cookie crumbs.

9. Refrigerate for 20 minutes to set and hydrate the cookie crumbs.

VARIATION: Rather than flavor the applesauce with mulling spices, try a combination of brown sugar, vanilla, and a touch of dark rum.

Per Serving: Calories: 362; Fat: 18g; Protein: 4g; Total carbohydrates: 48g; Fiber: 3g; Sugar: 23g; Sodium: 212mg

Key Lime Mousse

5-INGREDIENT • VEGETARIAN

Serves 6

Prep time: 10 minutes

Pressure cook: 10 minutes

Release: Natural (10 minutes), then quick

Chilling time: 2 hours

Total time: 2 hours 40 minutes

Based on the popular key lime pie, this easy mousse is tangy, light, and creamy. Nowadays, the tiny key limes can be hard to come by, so my recipe uses the juice and zest of the more common Persian limes. But plain old "lime mousse" seems boring, so "Key Lime Mousse" it is.

4 to 5 large Persian limes (or about 12 key limes)
¾ cup sugar
2 tablespoons unsalted butter, at room temperature

3 large eggs
Pinch kosher salt
1 cup water
1 cup chilled heavy cream

1. Grate the zest of 2 of the limes and set the zest aside. Cut all the limes in half and squeeze to get ½ cup of lime juice.

2. In a heatproof bowl that will fit in the inner pot, beat the sugar and butter with a hand mixer until the sugar has mostly dissolved and the mixture is light colored and fluffy. Add the eggs and beat until combined. Add the lime juice, lime zest, and salt and beat to combine. The mixture will appear grainy. Cover the bowl with foil.

3. Pour 1 cup water into the inner pot and insert a trivet with handles. Place the bowl on the trivet.

4. Lock the lid into place. Select Pressure Cook or Manual; adjust the pressure to High and the time to 10 minutes.

5. When cooking is complete, let the pressure release naturally for 10 minutes, then quick-release any remaining pressure. Remove the lid. Carefully lift out the bowl and trivet and remove the foil. The mixture will appear clumpy and curdled.

6. Whisk the curd mixture until smooth. Place a fine-mesh sieve over a medium bowl and pour the curd through it, pressing down with a flexible spatula to pass the curd through, leaving the zest and any curdled egg bits behind. Cover with plastic wrap, pushing the wrap down on top of the curd to keep a skin from forming. Refrigerate until well chilled, about 2 hours.

7. When the curd is chilled, whip the cream to medium-firm peaks. Add about one-third of the whipped cream to the curd and fold it in gently. Repeat with about half the remaining cream, then finish folding the cream into the curd with the last third.

8. Spoon into dessert dishes and serve immediately.

VARIATION: For a sour orange mousse, substitute ¼ cup each of lemon juice and orange juice for the lime juice, and use grated orange zest instead of the lime zest.

Per Serving: Calories: 318; Fat: 21g; Protein: 4g; Total carbohydrates: 32g; Fiber: 1.5g; Sugar: 26g; Sodium: 58mg

Easy Espresso Crème Caramel

5-INGREDIENT · VEGETARIAN

Serves 4

Prep time:
10 minutes

Pressure cook:
6 minutes

Release:
Natural
(10 minutes),
then quick

Cooling/ Chilling time: 2 hours 20 minutes

Total time:
3 hours
10 minutes

Like flan, crème caramel is a rich, eggy custard baked over a layer of caramel. Most recipes call for making the caramel specifically for the custard, but starting with store-bought caramel cuts down on the time and energy needed for this luscious dessert.

¼ cup Salted Caramel Sauce (page 153) or store-bought caramel sauce
1 tablespoon espresso powder
1 tablespoon very hot water
2 cups heavy cream
6 egg yolks
½ cup sugar
Pinch salt
1 cup water

1. Divide the caramel sauce evenly between four 1½-cup ramekins or custard cups. In a small bowl, dissolve the espresso powder in the hot water.

2. In a medium bowl, whisk together the cream and egg yolks until thoroughly combined. Whisk in the espresso mixture, sugar, and salt.

3. Pour the custard mixture into the ramekins or custard cups.

4. Add 1 cup water to the inner pot. Insert a trivet and place the ramekins on top, stacking if necessary. Drape a piece of foil over the ramekins.

5. Lock the lid into place. Select Pressure Cook or Manual; adjust the pressure to Low and the time to 6 minutes.

6. When cooking is complete, let the pressure release naturally for 10 minutes, then quick-release any remaining pressure. Remove the lid.

Continued >>

7. Carefully remove the foil and use tongs to remove the custards. Let cool at room temperature for 20 minutes or so, then refrigerate until chilled, about 2 hours.

8. To serve, run a knife or small spatula around the inside of the ramekins and invert the custards onto plates, scraping out any caramel that sticks.

VARIATION: For vanilla custard, omit the espresso powder and water, and add 1 teaspoon vanilla extract.

Per Serving: Calories: 655; Fat: 53g; Protein: 9g; Total carbohydrates: 39g; Fiber: 0g; Sugar: 38g; Sodium: 119mg

Dulce de Leche Rice Pudding

5-INGREDIENT • QUICK PREP • VEGETARIAN

Serves 6

Prep time:
5 minutes

Sauté:
5 minutes

Pressure cook:
12 minutes

Release:
Natural
(10 minutes),
then quick

Total time:
40 minutes

Dulce de leche, or caramelized sweetened condensed milk, is the key to this rich, delicious rice pudding. Cooking the rice in evaporated milk gives it an even creamier texture. For a thicker pudding, let it cool to room temperature before serving.

Cooking spray
1 cup arborio or long-grain white rice
1 (12-ounce) can evaporated milk, divided
1 cup water

Pinch kosher salt
1 cinnamon stick
1 cup sweetened condensed milk, or more to taste
1 (12-ounce) can dulce de leche

1. Mist the bottom of the inner pot with cooking spray. Add the rice, half of the evaporated milk, the water, the salt, and the cinnamon stick and stir together.

2. Lock the lid into place. Select Pressure Cook or Manual; adjust the pressure to Low and the time to 12 minutes.

3. When cooking is complete, let the pressure release naturally for 10 minutes, then quick-release any remaining pressure. Remove the lid. Remove the cinnamon stick.

4. Stir in the remaining half of the evaporated milk and the sweetened condensed milk. Taste and add more sweetened condensed milk if you prefer a sweeter pudding. Select Sauté and adjust the heat to Low. Bring the rice to a simmer and let cook for 5 to 10 minutes, until thickened to your taste.

5. Let cool slightly, then swirl in the dulce de leche and serve warm.

Per Serving: Calories: 557; Fat: 16g; Protein: 15g; Total carbohydrates: 91g; Fiber: 1.5g; Sugar: 62g; Sodium: 216mg

Staples

Restaurant-Style Salsa

DAIRY-FREE · QUICK PREP · VEGETARIAN

Makes 4 cups

This quick-cooking salsa is easy to make but big on flavor. Serve it with chips or on tacos, or use it in recipes such as Mexican-Inspired Shrimp Soup (page 68) or Huevos Rancheros with Refried Beans (page 24).

Prep time:
5 minutes

Pressure cook:
10 minutes

Release:
Natural (10 minutes), then quick

Cooling/ Chilling time: 1 hour 10 minutes

Total time:
1 hour 50 minutes

1 (28-ounce) can whole peeled tomatoes, undrained
1 green bell pepper, chopped
1 cup chopped onion
4 teaspoons minced garlic

½ cup chopped fresh cilantro
1 tablespoon fresh lime juice
1 teaspoon hot sauce, or more to taste
1 teaspoon kosher salt

1. In the inner pot, combine the tomatoes with their juices, bell pepper, onion, and garlic.

2. Lock the lid into place. Select Pressure Cook or Manual; adjust the pressure to High and the time to 10 minutes.

3. When cooking is complete, let the pressure release naturally for 10 minutes, then quick-release any remaining pressure.

4. Remove the lid. For a smoother texture, puree briefly with an immersion blender. Stir in the cilantro, lime juice, hot sauce, and salt. Let the salsa cool for about 10 minutes, then refrigerate it for 1 hour before serving.

   VARIATION: For a spicier salsa, substitute 2 to 3 jalapeños for the bell pepper.

Per Serving (¼ cup): Calories: 17; Fat: 0g; Protein: 0g; Total carbohydrates: 3g; Fiber: 0.5g; Sugar: 2g; Sodium: 147mg

Hot Pepper Sauce

5-INGREDIENT • **30-MINUTE** • **DAIRY-FREE** • **QUICK PREP** • **VEGETARIAN**

Makes
1¾ cups

Prep time:
3 minutes

Pressure cook:
2 minutes

Release:
Natural

Total time:
25 minutes

Did you know you can make your own hot pepper sauce? Like Tabasco or Crystal, but your own personal blend. It's surprising how easy it is to do. Just be careful—you may want to wear gloves while you prep the chiles (or at least wash your hands very thoroughly when you're done), and make sure to let the pressure release naturally all the way. You don't want to vent capsaicin vapor into the air.

12 to 16 ounces fresh red chiles, stemmed and halved

1 cup distilled white vinegar

¼ cup apple cider vinegar

3 garlic cloves, peeled and smashed

1. In the inner pot, stir together the chiles, distilled vinegar, apple cider vinegar, and garlic.

2. Lock the lid into place. Select Pressure Cook or Manual; adjust the pressure to High and the time to 2 minutes.

3. When cooking is complete, let the pressure release naturally. Carefully remove the lid, keeping your face away from the steam, which, depending on the spiciness of the peppers, can burn your sinuses.

4. Using an immersion blender, food processor, or blender, blend the sauce until smooth, again being careful not to inhale the vapor. Strain through a fine-mesh sieve, and store in glass bottles or jars at room temperature for up to 6 months.

VARIATION: For a smoky sauce, add one or two dried chipotle chiles to the fresh chiles.

Per Serving (1 teaspoon): Calories: 3; Fat: 0g; Protein: 0g; Total carbohydrates: 1g; Fiber: 0g; Sugar: 0.5g; Sodium: 1mg

Chicken Stock

5-INGREDIENT • 30-MINUTE • DAIRY-FREE • QUICK PREP

Makes 4 cups

Prep time:
5 minutes

Pressure cook: 1 hour 30 minutes

Release:
Natural (15 minutes), then quick

Chilling time:
8 hours

Total time:
10 hours

Though there are good chicken broths and stocks available in the grocery store, there's something special about making it from scratch: a silky texture from the collagen in the chicken bones. The Instant Pot makes it about as easy as can be. There's no need for skimming or simmering for half a day to get crystal-clear, delicious stock.

2 pounds meaty chicken bones (backs, wing tips, leg quarters)

1 small onion, peeled and halved through the root

1 bay leaf

¼ teaspoon kosher salt

3½ cups water

1. Place the chicken parts, onion, and bay leaf in the inner pot and sprinkle with the salt. Add the water; don't worry if it doesn't cover the bones.

2. Lock the lid into place. Select Pressure Cook or Manual; adjust the pressure to High and the time to 1 hour, 30 minutes.

3. When cooking is complete, let the pressure release naturally for 15 minutes, then quick-release any remaining pressure. Remove the lid.

4. Line a colander with cheesecloth and place it over a large bowl. Pour the chicken parts and stock into the colander to strain out the chicken and bones. Let the stock cool, then refrigerate for several hours or overnight so the fat hardens on the top of the stock.

5. Peel off the fat. The stock will last for several days in an airtight container in the refrigerator, or it can be frozen for up to 1 month.

Per Serving (½ cup): Calories: 10; Fat: 0g; Protein: 2g; Total carbohydrates: 0g; Fiber: 0g; Sugar: 0.5g; Sodium: 90mg

Vegetable Broth

5-INGREDIENT · 30-MINUTE · DAIRY-FREE · QUICK PREP · VEGETARIAN

Makes 4 cups

Prep time:
5 minutes

Sauté:
5 minutes

Pressure cook:
45 minutes

Release:
Natural
(15 minutes),
then quick

Total time:
1 hour
30 minutes

I'm not a big fan of most commercial vegetable broths; they can be oddly sweet or too bitter. This recipe yields a quart of complex, savory broth that's perfect as a base for vegetarian soups or stews.

1 tablespoon vegetable oil
1 cup sliced onion
1 pound sliced button or
  cremini mushrooms

2 large carrots, peeled and cut
  into 1-inch pieces
¼ teaspoon kosher salt
3½ cups water

1. Select Sauté and adjust the heat to High. Add the oil until shimmering or the display reads "Hot." Add the onion and cook, stirring occasionally, until quite browned but not charred, 4 to 5 minutes.

2. Add the mushrooms and carrots to the inner pot and sprinkle with the salt. Add the water and stir to combine.

3. Lock the lid into place. Select Pressure Cook or Manual; adjust the pressure to High and the time to 45 minutes.

4. When cooking is complete, let the pressure release naturally for 15 minutes, then quick-release any remaining pressure. Remove the lid.

5. Place a colander or fine-mesh sieve over a large bowl. Pour the vegetables and stock into the colander. Discard the solids. Let cool to room temperature, then refrigerate. The stock can be refrigerated for several days or frozen for several months in airtight containers.

Per Serving (½ cup): Calories: 17; Fat: 1.5g; Protein: 0g; Total carbohydrates: 0g; Fiber: 0g; Sugar: 0.5g; Sodium: 40mg

Yogurt

5-INGREDIENT • QUICK PREP • VEGETARIAN

Makes 4 cups

Prep time:
5 minutes

Yogurt:
8 hours
20 minutes

Chilling time:
4 hours

Total time:
12 hours
30 minutes

Though making yogurt at home does take time, it's almost all hands-off, and the results are fantastic. Start with a tablespoon of leftover yogurt for your first batch, and then you can use your own for future batches.

1 quart whole milk

1 tablespoon plain whole-milk yogurt with live cultures, at room temperature

1. Pour the milk into the inner pot. Select Yogurt and press adjust so that BOIL shows in the display. Lock the lid into place. When the beeper sounds, unlock the lid. Use a thermometer to take the temperature of the milk in the center of the pot. It should read between 179°F and 182°F. This should take about 20 minutes.

2. Fill a large bowl or the sink with ice water and place the inner pot in it to cool. Stir the milk occasionally, without scraping the bottom of the pot, for about 3 minutes, then take the temperature in the center of the milk. It should read between 110° and 115°F. Remove the pot from the ice bath and dry off the outside of the pot. Return the pot to the base.

3. In a small bowl, stir together the yogurt and about ½ cup of the warm milk. Add the yogurt mixture to the pot and stir thoroughly but gently. Again, don't scrape the bottom of the pot (if there is any coagulated milk on the bottom, stirring it in can make your yogurt less smooth).

4. Lock the lid into place (or use a glass lid) and select Yogurt. The display should read 8:00, which indicates 8 hours of incubation time. If you prefer a longer incubation, press the + button to increase the time by increments of 30 minutes.

Continued >>

5. When the yogurt cycle is complete, remove the inner pot and cover it with a glass or silicone lid, or place a plate on top. Refrigerate until chilled, about 4 hours, before using or stirring.

6. If you'd like to make Greek yogurt, line a colander or large sieve with cheesecloth. Place the colander over a large bowl. Spoon the yogurt into the colander and let drain for 15 to 30 minutes, depending on how thick you want your yogurt.

SUBSTITUTION TIP: If you like, you can substitute low-fat (1%) milk, but avoid fat-free milk; it doesn't set up well.

Per Serving (½ cup): Calories: 75; Fat: 4g; Protein: 4g; Total carbohydrates: 6g; Fiber: 0g; Sugar: 6g; Sodium: 53mg

Marinara Sauce

5-INGREDIENT • DAIRY-FREE • QUICK PREP • VEGETARIAN

Makes about 4 cups

Having homemade marinara sauce on hand makes it simple to create delicious Italian meals any night of the week. With only a few ingredients, you can make a sauce to rival your favorite store-bought brand.

Prep time:
5 minutes

Sauté:
5 minutes

Pressure cook:
15 minutes

Release:
Natural
(10 minutes),
then quick

Cooling time:
10 minutes

Total time:
55 minutes

3 tablespoons extra-virgin olive oil
1 cup chopped onion
1 tablespoon minced garlic
1 (28-ounce) can crushed tomatoes

2 tablespoons tomato paste
1 teaspoon Italian seasoning
1 teaspoon kosher salt, plus more to taste

1. Select Sauté and adjust the heat to High. Add the oil to the inner pot and heat until shimmering or the display reads "Hot." Add the onion and garlic and cook, stirring, for 2 to 3 minutes, until the vegetables have started to soften.

2. Pour in the crushed tomatoes and stir to combine, scraping the bottom of the pot if there is anything stuck. Stir in the tomato paste, Italian seasoning and salt.

3. Lock the lid into place. Select Pressure Cook or Manual; adjust the pressure to High and the time to 15 minutes.

4. When cooking is complete, let the pressure release naturally for 10 minutes, then quick-release any remaining pressure. Remove the lid.

5. Let the sauce cool for about 10 minutes, then taste and adjust the seasoning, adding more salt if necessary. Refrigerate for up to a week or freeze for 4 to 6 weeks.

Per Serving (½ cup): Calories: 91; Fat: 5g; Protein: 2g; Total carbohydrates: 10g; Fiber: 3g; Sugar: 5g; Sodium: 354mg

Salted Caramel Sauce

5-INGREDIENT • QUICK PREP • VEGETARIAN

Makes about 2 cups

Prep time:
5 minutes

Pressure cook:
45 minutes

Release:
Natural

Total time:
1 hour
15 minutes

I love caramel sauce, but I hate to make it on the stovetop. It's so easy to ruin by stirring it at the wrong time or not stirring it at the right time. This method makes it virtually foolproof, and it produces a delicious, creamy sauce you won't be able to resist.

1 (14-ounce) can sweetened condensed milk
1 tablespoon unsalted butter
½ teaspoon vanilla extract
½ teaspoon kosher salt
¼ cup heavy cream

1. Pour the sweetened condensed milk into a deep 2-cup bowl or measuring cup and crimp foil over the top. Place the cup in the inner pot and add water to reach the level of the milk in the cup.

2. Lock the lid into place. Select Pressure Cook or Manual; adjust the pressure to High and the time to 45 minutes.

3. When cooking is complete, let the pressure release naturally. Remove the lid.

4. Lift the measuring cup out of the pot and remove the foil. Add the butter, vanilla, salt, and cream to the measuring cup. Use an immersion blender to blend the sauce until it's smooth. Use right away or refrigerate for several weeks, warming it to thin it out before using.

   VARIATION: For a chocolate caramel sauce, omit the butter and salt and stir in 3 ounces of chopped dark chocolate.

Per Serving (2 tablespoons): Calories: 127; Fat: 5g; Protein: 3g; Total carbohydrates: 18g; Fiber: 0g; Sugar: 18g; Sodium: 78mg

Barbecue Sauce

30-MINUTE • DAIRY-FREE • QUICK PREP

Makes about 2 cups

Prep time:
5 minutes

Pressure cook:
8 minutes

Release:
Natural (5 minutes), then quick

Total time:
30 minutes

I first tried my hand at making barbecue sauce years ago, from a recipe I found in a magazine. It called for roasting tomatoes and onions, toasting and rehydrating dried chiles, simmering for a couple of hours, and pureeing in a blender. It was good, but a lot of work. I've kept the flavor but streamlined the process, so this delicious sauce is ready in half an hour. For a spicier sauce, increase the amount of chipotle.

1½ cups canned tomato sauce
1 teaspoon kosher salt
2 teaspoons minced garlic
½ cup sliced onion
1 tablespoon ancho chile powder
1 teaspoon chipotle powder

½ teaspoon freshly ground black pepper
1 teaspoon Worcestershire sauce
1 tablespoon apple cider vinegar
2 tablespoons light brown sugar

1. Place the tomato sauce, salt, garlic, onion, ancho powder, chipotle powder, pepper, Worcestershire sauce, vinegar, and brown sugar in the inner pot.

2. Lock the lid into place. Select Pressure Cook or Manual; adjust the pressure to High and the time to 8 minutes.

3. When cooking is complete, let the pressure release naturally for 5 minutes, then quick-release any remaining pressure. Remove the lid.

4. Let cool for a few minutes, then use an immersion blender to puree. Refrigerate for a week or freeze for up to 1 month.

   SUBSTITUTION TIP: If you can't find ancho chile powder, substitute chili powder.

Per Serving (2 tablespoons): Calories: 16; Fat: 0g; Protein: 0g; Total carbohydrates: 4g; Fiber: 0g; Sugar: 3g; Sodium: 202mg

MEASUREMENT CONVERSIONS

VOLUME EQUIVALENTS	U.S. STANDARD	U.S. STANDARD (OUNCES)	METRIC (APPROXIMATE)
LIQUID	2 tablespoons	1 fl. oz.	30 mL
	¼ cup	2 fl. oz.	60 mL
	½ cup	4 fl. oz.	120 mL
	1 cup	8 fl. oz.	240 mL
	1½ cups	12 fl. oz.	355 mL
	2 cups or 1 pint	16 fl. oz.	475 mL
	4 cups or 1 quart	32 fl. oz.	1 L
	1 gallon	128 fl. oz.	4 L
DRY	⅛ teaspoon	—	0.5 mL
	¼ teaspoon	—	1 mL
	½ teaspoon	—	2 mL
	¾ teaspoon	—	4 mL
	1 teaspoon	—	5 mL
	1 tablespoon	—	15 mL
	¼ cup	—	59 mL
	⅓ cup	—	79 mL
	½ cup	—	118 mL
	⅔ cup	—	156 mL
	¾ cup	—	177 mL
	1 cup	—	235 mL
	2 cups or 1 pint	—	475 mL
	3 cups	—	700 mL
	4 cups or 1 quart	—	1 L
	½ gallon	—	2 L
	1 gallon	—	4 L

OVEN TEMPERATURES

FAHRENHEIT	CELSIUS (APPROXIMATE)
250°F	120°C
300°F	150°C
325°F	165°C
350°F	180°C
375°F	190°C
400°F	200°C
425°F	220°C
450°F	230°C

WEIGHT EQUIVALENTS

U.S. STANDARD	METRIC (APPROXIMATE)
½ ounce	15 g
1 ounce	30 g
2 ounces	60 g
4 ounces	115 g
8 ounces	225 g
12 ounces	340 g
16 ounces or 1 pound	455 g

INSTANT POT PRESSURE COOKING TIME CHARTS

The following charts provide approximate times for a variety of foods. To begin, you may want to cook for a minute or two less than the times listed; you can always simmer foods at natural pressure to finish cooking.

Keep in mind that these times are for the foods partially submerged in water (or broth) or steamed, and for the foods cooked alone. The cooking times for the same foods when they are part of a recipe may differ because of additional ingredients or cooking liquids, or a different release method than the one listed here.

For any foods labeled with "natural" release, allow at least 15 minutes natural pressure release before quick releasing any remaining pressure.

Beans and Legumes

If you are cooking 1 pound or more of beans, it's best to use low pressure and increase the cooking time by a minute or two (with larger amounts, there's more chance for foaming at high pressure). If you have less than 1 pound, high pressure is fine. A little oil in the cooking liquid will reduce foaming. Unless a shorter release time is indicated, let the beans release naturally for at least 15 minutes, after which any remaining pressure can be quick released. Beans should be soaked in salted water for 8 to 24 hours before cooking, unless otherwise noted.

	LIQUID PER 1 CUP OF BEANS	MINUTES UNDER PRESSURE	PRESSURE	RELEASE
BLACK BEANS	2 cups	8 / 9	High / Low	Natural
BLACK-EYED PEAS	2 cups	5	High	Natural for 8 minutes, then quick
CANNELLINI BEANS	2 cups	5 / 7	High / Low	Natural
CHICKPEAS (GARBANZO BEANS)	2 cups	4	High	Natural for 3 minutes, then quick
KIDNEY BEANS	2 cups	5 / 7	High / Low	Natural
BROWN LENTILS (UNSOAKED)	2¼ cups	20	High	Natural for 10 minutes, then quick
RED LENTILS (UNSOAKED)	3 cups	10	High	Natural for 5 minutes, then quick
PINTO BEANS	2 cups	8 / 10	High / Low	Natural
SPLIT PEAS (UNSOAKED)	3 cups	5 (firm peas) to 8 (soft peas)	High	Natural
LIMA BEANS	2 cups	4 / 5	High / Low	Natural for 5 minutes, then quick
SOY BEANS, FRESH (EDAMAME, UNSOAKED)	1 cup	1	High	Quick
SOYBEANS, DRIED	2 cups	12 / 14	High / Low	Natural

Grains

To prevent foaming, it's best to rinse these grains thoroughly before cooking, or include a small amount of butter or oil with the cooking liquid. Unless a shorter release time is indicated, let the grains release naturally for at least 15 minutes, after which any remaining pressure can be quick released.

	LIQUID PER 1 CUP OF GRAIN	MINUTES UNDER PRESSURE	PRESSURE	RELEASE
ARBORIO RICE (FOR RISOTTO)	3–4 cups	6–8	High	Quick
BARLEY, PEARLED	2½ cups	20	High	Natural for 10 minutes, then quick
BROWN RICE, MEDIUM GRAIN	1 cup	12	High	Natural
BROWN RICE, LONG GRAIN	1 cup	22	High	Natural for 10 minutes, then quick
BUCKWHEAT	1¾ cups	2–4	High	Natural
FARRO, WHOLE GRAIN	3 cups	22–24	High	Natural
FARRO, PEARLED	2 cups	6–8	High	Natural
OATS, ROLLED	3 cups	3–4	High	Quick
OATS, STEEL CUT	3 cups	10	High	Natural for 10 minutes, then quick
QUINOA	1 cup	2	High	Natural for 12 minutes, then quick
WHEAT BERRIES	2 cups	30	High	Natural for 10 minutes, then quick
WHITE RICE, LONG GRAIN	1 cup	3	High	Natural
WILD RICE	1¼ cups	22–24	High	Natural

Meat

Except as noted, these times are for braised meats—that is, meats that are seared before pressure cooking and partially submerged in liquid. Unless a shorter release time is indicated, let the meat release naturally for at least 15 minutes, after which any remaining pressure can be quick released.

	MINUTES UNDER PRESSURE	PRESSURE	RELEASE
BEEF, SHOULDER (CHUCK) ROAST (2 LB.)	35–45	High	Natural
BEEF, SHOULDER (CHUCK), 2" CHUNKS	20	High	Natural for 10 minutes
BEEF, BONE-IN SHORT RIBS	40	High	Natural
BEEF, FLAT IRON STEAK, CUT INTO ½" STRIPS	6	Low	Quick
BEEF, SIRLOIN STEAK, CUT INTO ½" STRIPS	3	Low	Quick
LAMB, SHOULDER, 2" CHUNKS	35	High	Natural
LAMB, SHANKS	40	High	Natural
PORK, SHOULDER ROAST (2 LB.)	25	High	Natural
PORK, SHOULDER, 2" CHUNKS	20	High	Quick
PORK, TENDERLOIN	4	Low	Quick
PORK, BACK RIBS (STEAMED)	25	High	Quick
PORK, SPARE RIBS (STEAMED)	20	High	Quick
PORK, SMOKED SAUSAGE, ½" SLICES	5–10	High	Quick

Poultry

Except as noted, these times are for braised poultry—that is, partially submerged in liquid. Unless a shorter release time is indicated, let the poultry release naturally for at least 15 minutes, after which any remaining pressure can be quick released.

	MINUTES UNDER PRESSURE	PRESSURE	RELEASE
CHICKEN BREAST, BONE-IN (STEAMED)	8	Low	Natural for 5 minutes
CHICKEN BREAST, BONELESS (STEAMED)	5	Low	Natural for 8 minutes
CHICKEN THIGH, BONE-IN	10–14	High	Natural for 10 minutes
CHICKEN THIGH, BONELESS	6–8	High	Natural for 10 minutes
CHICKEN THIGH, BONELESS, 1"–2" PIECES	5–6	High	Quick
CHICKEN, WHOLE (SEARED ON ALL SIDES)	12–14	Low	Natural for 8 minutes
DUCK QUARTERS, BONE-IN	35	High	Quick
TURKEY BREAST, TENDERLOIN (12 OZ.) (STEAMED)	5	Low	Natural for 8 minutes
TURKEY THIGH, BONE-IN	30	High	Natural

Fish and Seafood

All times are for steamed fish and shellfish.

	MINUTES UNDER PRESSURE	PRESSURE	RELEASE
CLAMS	2	High	Quick
MUSSELS	1	High	Quick
SALMON, FRESH (1" THICK)	5	Low	Quick
HALIBUT, FRESH (1" THICK)	3	High	Quick
TILAPIA OR COD, FRESH	1	Low	Quick
TILAPIA OR COD, FROZEN	3	Low	Quick
LARGE SHRIMP, FROZEN	1	Low	Quick

Vegetables

The cooking method for all the following vegetables is steaming; if the vegetables are cooked in liquid, the times may vary. Green vegetables will be tender-crisp; root vegetables will be soft. Unless a shorter release time is indicated, let the vegetables release naturally for at least 15 minutes, after which any remaining pressure can be quick released.

	PREP	MINUTES UNDER PRESSURE	PRESSURE	RELEASE
ACORN SQUASH	Halved	9	High	Quick
ARTICHOKES, LARGE	Whole	15	High	Quick
BEETS	Quartered if large; halved if small	9	High	Natural
BROCCOLI	Cut into florets	1	Low	Quick
BRUSSELS SPROUTS	Halved	2	High	Quick
BUTTERNUT SQUASH	Peeled, ½" chunks	8	High	Quick
CABBAGE	Sliced	3–4	High	Quick
CARROTS	½"–1" slices	2	High	Quick
CAULIFLOWER	Whole	6	High	Quick
CAULIFLOWER	Cut into florets	1	Low	Quick
GREEN BEANS	Cut in halves or thirds	3	Low	Quick
POTATOES, LARGE RUSSET (FOR MASHING)	Quartered	8	High	Natural for 8 minutes, then quick
POTATOES, RED	Whole if less than 1½" across, halved if larger	4	High	Quick
SPAGHETTI SQUASH	Halved lengthwise	7	High	Quick
SWEET POTATOES	Halved lengthwise	8	High	Natural

INDEX

Acknowledgments

Many thanks to the team at Rockridge Press, especially Van Van Cleave, Ashley Popp, and Bowie Rowan. Thanks also to Lauren Keating, Kristen Greazel, Felicia Slattery, and Carrie Forrest, whose recipes appear in these chapters.

About the Author

JANET A. ZIMMERMAN is an award-winning food writer and former cooking teacher. She is the author or editor of 13 previous cookbooks, including the best-selling *Instant Pot Obsession*. She lives near Atlanta with her partner, Dave.